the

# German
Travelmate

compiled by
**Lexus**
with
**Ingrid Schumacher**
and
**Sigrid Köhler**

LEXUS

This new edition published 2004 by Lexus Ltd
60 Brook Street, Glasgow G40 2AB
Maps drawn by András Bereznay
Typeset by Elfreda Crehan
Series editor: Peter Terrell

First published in 1982 by Richard Drew Publishing Ltd,
ISBN 0-904002-75-6
Published in 1991 by W & R Chambers Ltd, ISBN 0-550-
22001-1


British Library Cataloguing in Publication Data
A catalogue record for this book is available from the
British Library.

ISBN 1-904737-02-1


Printed and bound in Great Britain by Scotprint

## Your Travelmate

gives you one single easy-to-use A to Z list of words and phrases to help you communicate in German.

Built into this list are:

- travel tips (✈) with facts and figures which provide valuable information
- German words you'll see on signs and notices
- typical replies to some of the things you might want to say
- language notes giving you basic information about speaking the language
- a menu reader on pages 84-87

There are maps of Germany, Austria and Switzerland on pages 156-158. Numbers and the German alphabet are on pages 159-160.

## Speaking German

Your Travelmate also tells you how to pronounce German. Just read the pronunciation guides given in square brackets as though they were English and you will communicate – although you might not sound exactly like a native speaker.

If no pronunciation is given then this is because the German word itself can be spoken more or less as though it were English.

Sometimes only a part of a word or phrase needs a pronunciation guide.

### Stress

Letters in blue show which part of a word to stress, or to give more weight to, when speaking German. Getting the stress right is particularly important.

Some special points about the pronunciation system used to represent German:

| | |
|---|---|
| ah | like the a in father |
| air | like the air sound in hair |
| ay | like the ay in pay |
| gh | like the g in go |
| I | like the i in hi |
| J | like the s in leisure |
| KH | at the back of the throat, like ch in the way Scots pronounce loch (or think of Bach) |
| oo | like the oo in boot |
| ∞ | like the oo in foot, a shorter sound |
| ōō | like the u in huge or the u in French du |
| ow | like the ow in cow |
| SH | try saying sh but with the sides of your tongue curled up against your teeth |
| uh | like the e in fitter |
| ur | like the u in purr but with no r sound |
| y | like the y in why |

ine, ite etc are ways of showing the common German sound ei (think of Einstein).

## Men and women speaking

When you see an entry like:

**next of kin** der/die nächste Angehörige [nekstuh an-gheh-hur-iguh]

the German given after the slash is the form to be used for women. So a man would be:

**next of kin** der nächste Angehörige

and a woman would be:

**next of kin** die nächste Angehörige

## Language backup

To find out more about Lexus and Lexus Translations or to comment on this book you can go on-line to www.lexusforlanguages.co.uk.

# A [ah]

**a, an** ein/eine/ein [ine/ine-uh...]

> The corresponding words for 'the' are
> **der/die/das**.

**Abfahrt** departures
**about: is he about?** ist er da? [...air...]
   **about 15** ungefähr fünfzehn [oon-gheh-fair foonf-tsayn]
   **about 2 o'clock** gegen zwei Uhr [gay-ghen tsvy oor]
**above** über [ōober]
**abroad** im Ausland [im owss-lant]
**absolutely!** genau! [gheh-now]
**accelerator** das Gas [gahss]
**accept** annehmen [an-nay-men]
**accident** der Unfall [oonfal]
   **there's been an accident** es ist ein Unfall passiert [...pas-eert]
**accurate** genau [gheh-now]
**Achtung** caution, danger; (*spoken*) look out!, (*announcement*) attention please
**across** über [ōober]
   **it's across the street** es ist auf der anderen Straßenseite [...owf dair anderen shtrahssen-zytuh]
**ADAC, Allgemeiner Deutscher Automobil-Club** equivalent of AA, RAC
**adaptor** der Zwischenstecker [tsvishen-shtecker]
**address** die Adresse [ad-ressuh]
   **will you give me your address?** würden Sie mir Ihre Adresse geben? [vōorden zee meer eer-uh ad-ressuh gay-ben]
**adjust** einstellen [ine-shtellen]
**admission** der Eintritt [ine-]

**advance: can we book in advance?** können
wir *im Voraus* buchen? [kurnen veer im for-owss
booкнen]

**advert** die Annonce [a-non-suh]

**afraid: I'm afraid so** ja, leider [...ly-der]

**I'm afraid not** leider nicht [...nisHt]

**after** nach [nahкн]

**after you** nach Ihnen [nahкн ee-nen]

**afternoon** der Nachmittag [nahкн-mitahg]

**in the afternoon** nachmittags

**this afternoon** heute nachmittag [hoytuh...]

**aftershave** das Rasierwasser [raz-eer-vasser]

**again** wieder [veeder]

**against** gegen [gay-ghen]

**age** das Alter [al-ter]

**under age** minderjährig [minnder-yair-risH]

**it takes ages** das dauert eine Ewigkeit [...
dowert ine-uh ay-visH-kite]

**ago: a week ago** *vor* einer Woche [for ine-ner
voкн-uh]

**it wasn't long ago** das ist noch nicht lange her
[dass ist noкн nisHt lang-uh hair]

**how long ago was that?** wie lange ist das her?
[vee...]

**agree: I agree** da stimme ich zu [...shtim-uh isH
tsoo]

**it doesn't agree with me** das bekommt mir
nicht [...buh-kommt meer nisHt]

**air** die Luft [lœft]

**by air** per Flugzeug [pair floog-tsoyg]

**air-conditioning: with air-conditioning** mit
Klimaanlage [...kleema-an-lahguh]

**air hostess** die Hostess

**airmail: by airmail** per Luftpost [pair lœft-posst]

**airport** der Flughafen [floog-hahfen]

**does this go to the airport?** fährt der zum
Flughafen? [fairt dair tsœm...]

**airport bus** der Flughafenbus [floog-hahfen-booss]

**aisle seat** ein Sitz am Gang [zits...]

**alarm clock** der Wecker [v-]

**alcohol** der Alkohol [alkohohl]
  **is it alcoholic?** ist das Alkohol?

**alive: is he still alive?** *lebt* er noch? [laybt air noкн]

**all: all the people** alle Leute [al-uh loytuh]
  **all night/all day** die ganze Nacht/den ganzen Tag [dee gants-uh nahкнt/dayn gants-en tahg]

**all** *(everything)* alles [al-ess]
  **that's all** das ist alles
  **that's all wrong** das ist *ganz* falsch
  **thank you – not at all** danke – bitte [...bittuh]
  **all right** in Ordnung! [...ordnoong]
  **I'm all right** es geht mir gut [ess gayt meer goot]

**allergic: I'm allergic to...** ich bin allergisch gegen... [al-air-ghish gay-ghen]

**allowed: is it allowed?** darf man das?
  **that's not allowed** das ist verboten [...fair-bohten]
  **allow me** gestatten Sie mir [gheh-shtaten zee meer]

**almost** fast [fasst]

**alone** allein [al-ine]
  **did you come here alone?** sind Sie allein hier? [zinnt zee...heer]
  **leave me alone** lassen Sie mich in Ruhe [...zee misн in roo-uh]

**Alps** die Alpen

**already** schon [shohn]

**also** auch [owкн]

**although** obwohl [ob-vohl]

**altogether** insgesamt [inss-gheh-zammt]
  **what does that make altogether?** was macht

das zusammen? [vass mahкнt dass tsoo-zammen]

**always** immer

**am**[1] *go to* **be**

**am**[2] *(in the morning)* morgens [mor-ghens]

> ✈ The 24-hour clock is commonly used in spoken German.

**ambulance** ein Krankenwagen [kranken-vah-ghen]
  **get an ambulance!** rufen Sie einen Krankenwagen! [roo-fen zee ine-en...]

> ✈ Dial 110.

**America** Amerika [amay-reeka]
**American** *(man)* ein Amerikaner [amayree-kahner]
  *(woman)* eine Amerikanerin
  *(adjective)* amerikanisch
**among** unter [oonter]
**amp: a 13-amp fuse** eine Sicherung von dreizehn Ampere [zisheroong fon...am-pair]
**and** und [oont]
**angry** böse [bur-zuh]
  **I'm very angry (about it)** ich bin deswegen sehr verärgert [...dess-vay-ghen zair fair-air-ghert]
**ankle** der Fußknöchel [fooss-knur-sнel]
**Ankauf** buying rate
**Ankunft** arrivals
**Anlieger frei** residents only
**Anmeldung** reception
**anniversary: it's our anniversary** heute ist unser *Hochzeitstag* [hoytuh ist oon-ser hoкн-tsites-tahg]
**annoy: he's annoying me** er belästigt mich [air belestisнt misн]
  **it's very annoying** das ist sehr ärgerlich [dass ist zair air-gherlisн]
**anorak** der Anorak
**another: can we have another room?** können

wir *ein anderes* Zimmer haben? [kurnen veer ine an-dress tsimmer hah-ben]

**another beer, please** noch ein Bier, bitte [noкн ine beer bittuh]

**answer** die Antwort [ant-vort]

**what was his answer?** was hat er darauf geantwortet? [vass hat air darowf gheh-ant-vortet]

**there was no answer** es hat sich niemand gemeldet [...zisн nee-mant gheh-meldet]

**antibiotics** Antibiotika [antee-bee-otika]

**antifreeze** das Frostschutzmittel [frost-shoots-mittel]

**any: have you got any bananas/butter?** haben Sie Bananen/Butter? [hah-ben zee banah-nen/bœ-ter]

**we haven't got any money/rolls** wir haben kein Geld/keine Brötchen [...kine/kine-uh...]

**I haven't got any** *(of one thing)* ich habe keins [...kine-ss]

**I haven't got any** *(of several things)* ich habe keine

**anybody** (irgend) jemand [eer-ghent yay-mant]

**we don't know anybody** wir kennen niemanden [...nee-manden]

**anything** (irgend)etwas [eer-ghent et-vass]

**I don't want anything** ich möchte gar nichts [isн mursнtuh gar nisнts]

**apology: please accept my apologies** bitte, verzeihen Sie mir [bittuh fair-tsy-en zee meer]

**appendicitis** eine Blinddarmentzündung [blint-darm-ent-tsœn-dœng]

**appetite** der Appetit [-teet]

**I've lost my appetite** ich habe keinen Appetit mehr [isн hah-buh kine-en...mair]

**apple** ein Apfel

**apple pie** ein Apfelkuchen [apfel-kooкнen]

**appointment: can I make an appointment?**
könnte ich einen *Termin* ausmachen? [kurntuh
isн ine-en tairmeen owss-mahкнen]
**apricot** eine Aprikose [ap-ree-kohzuh]
**April** April [apreel]
**are** *go to* **be**
**area** *(neighbourhood)* die Gegend [gay-ghent]
*(space)* der Raum [rowm]
**area code** die Vorwahl [for-vahl]

✈ If you're in Germany you have to include
the zero of the area code. But not if calling
from abroad.

**arm** der Arm
**around** *go to* **about**
**arrange: will you arrange it?** können Sie das
arrangieren? [kurnen zee dass ar-ron-Jee-ren]
**arrest** verhaften [fair-haff-ten]
**arrival** die Ankunft [an-koonft]
**arrive** ankommen
**we only arrived yesterday** wir sind erst gestern
angekommen [veer zint airst ghestern...]
**art** die Kunst [koonst]
**art gallery** eine Kunstgalerie [koonst-]
**arthritis** die Arthritis [ar-tree-tis]
**artificial** künstlich [koonstlisн]
**artist** der Künstler [koonstler]
*(woman)* die Künstlerin
**as: as quickly as you can** so schnell Sie können
[zo shnel zee kurnen]
**as much as you can** so viel Sie können
[...feel...]
**as you like** wie Sie wollen [vee zee vollen]
**ashore** an Land [an lant]
**ashtray** der Aschenbecher [ashen-besнer]
**ask** fragen [frah-ghen]
**could you ask him to...?** könnten Sie ihn

bitten, zu… [kurnten zee een bit-en tsoo]
**that's not what I asked for** das habe ich nicht
bestellt [dass hah-buh ish nisht buh-shtellt]
**asleep: he's still asleep** er schläft noch [air shlayft
nokh]
**asparagus** der Spargel [shpargel]
**aspirin** eine Kopfschmerztablette [kopf-shmairts-
tab-lettuh]
**assistant** *(in shop)* der Verkäufer [fair-koy-fer]
*(woman)* die Verkäuferin
**asthma** das Asthma [astma]
**at: at the airport** am Flughafen
**at my hotel** in meinem Hotel
**at one o'clock** um ein Uhr [oom…]
**at Michael's** bei Michael [by…]
**attitude** die Einstellung [ine-shtel-oong]
**attractive: I think you're very attractive** ich
finde Sie sehr attraktiv [ish fin-duh zee zair
atrakteef]
**aubergine** die Aubergine [o-bair-Jeenuh]
**Aufzug** lift
**August** August [ow-goost]
**aunt: my aunt** meine Tante [mine-uh tant-uh]
**Ausfahrt** exit
**Ausfahrt freihalten** exit: keep clear
**Ausgang** exit
**Auskunft** information
**Ausland** abroad, overseas
**außer Betrieb** out of order
**Australia** Australien [owss-trah-lee-un]
**Austria** Österreich [ur-ster-rysh]
**Austrian** österreichisch [ur-ster-ryshish]
*(man)* der Österreicher [ur-ster-rysher]
*(woman)* die Österreicherin
**Ausverkauf** sale
**ausverkauft** sold out
**authorities** die Behörden [buh-hurden]

**automatic** automatisch [owto-mahtish]
  (car) ein Automatikwagen [owto-mahtik-vah-ghen]
**autumn: in the autumn** im Herbst [im hairpst]
**away: is it far away from here?** ist es weit von hier? [ist ess vite fon heer]
  **go away!** geh weg! [gay vek]
**awful** schrecklich [shreck-lish]
**axle** die Achse [ak-suh]

# B [bay]

**baby** ein Baby
  **we'd like a baby-sitter** wir brauchen einen Babysitter [veer browⲕнen ine-en...]
**back: I've got a bad back** ich habe Schwierigkeiten mit meinem *Rücken* [ish hah-buh shvee-rish-kite-en mit mine-em rⲟⲟcken]
  **at the back** hinten
  **I'll be right back** ich bin gleich wieder da [ish bin glysн veeder da]
  **is he back?** ist er wieder da?
  **can I have my money back?** kann ich mein Geld wiederhaben? [kann ish mine ghelt veeder-hah-ben]
  **I go back tomorrow** ich fahre morgen *zurück* [ish fahr-ruh mor-ghen tsoo-rⲟⲟck]
**backpacker** der Rucksacktourist [rⲟⲟck-zack-]
  (female) die Rucksacktouristin
**bacon** der Speck [shpeck]
  **bacon and eggs** Eier mit Speck [ɪ-er...]
**bad** schlecht [shlesнt]
  **it's not bad** nicht schlecht [nisнt...]
  **too bad!** Pech! [pesн]
**Bad** bathroom
**Baden verboten** no bathing
**bag** eine Tasche [tash-uh]

*(suitcase)* eine Reisetasche [ry-zuh-]
*(from shop)* eine Tüte [tootuh]
**baggage** das Gepäck [gheh-peck]
**Bahnsteig** platform
**Bahnübergang** level crossing
**baker's** der Bäcker [becker]
**balcony** der Balkon [bal-kohn]
  **a room with a balcony** ein Zimmer mit Balkon
  [ine tsimmer...]
**bald: he's bald** er hat eine Glatze [...ine-uh glats-
  uh]
**ball** *(football etc)* der Ball [bal]
**ball-point (pen)** ein Kugelschreiber [kooghel-
  shryber]
**banana** eine Banane [banahnuh]
**band** *(musical)* die Kapelle [-elluh]
  *(pop)* eine Band [bant]
**bandage** die Binde [bin-duh]
  **could you change the bandage?** könnten Sie
  den Verband wechseln? [kurnten zee dayn fair-
  bant vekseln]
**bank** *(for money)* die Bank

> ✈ Open 9-16.30. Smaller branches close
> 12.30-14.00 and Wednesday afternoons;
> some banks open until 18.00 on Thursday.

**bank holiday** *go to* **public holidays**
**bar** die Bar
  **in the bar** in der Bar

> *YOU MAY HEAR*
> was darf's sein? *what will you have?*

> ✈ In bars and pubs it's usual to pay when
> you leave, not when you are served. Table
> service is standard.

**barber's** der (Herren)friseur [(hairen-)free-zur]

**bargain: it's a real bargain** das ist wirklich günstig [dass ist virk-lisH gōōn-stisH]

**barmaid** die Bardame [bar-dahm-uh]

**barman** der Barkeeper

**baseball cap** eine Baseballmütze [-mōōts-uh]

**basket** der Korb [korp]

**bath** das Bad [baht]

  **can I have a bath?** kann ich ein Bad nehmen? [kann isH ine baht nay-men]

  **could you give me a bath towel?** könnten Sie mir ein Badetuch geben? [kurnten zee meer ine bah-duh-tooкн gay-ben]

**bathroom** das Badezimmer [bah-duh-tsimmer]

  **we want a room with bathroom** wir hätten gerne ein Zimmer mit Bad [veer hetten gair-nuh ine tsimmer mit baht]

  **can I use your bathroom?** könnte ich Ihre Toilette benutzen? [kurntuh isH eer-uh twalet-uh buh-nootsen]

**battery** die Batterie [bat-eree]

**be** sein [zine]

> Here is the present tense of the German for 'to be'.
>
> **I am** ich bin [isH...]
> **you are** (familiar) du bist [doo...]
> **you are** (polite) Sie sind [zee zint]
> **he/she/it is** er/sie/es ist [air/zee/ess...]
> **we are** wir sind [veer...]
> **you are** (familiar plural) ihr seid [eer zite]
> **you are** (polite plural) Sie sind
> **they are** sie sind

**be reasonable** seien Sie vernünftig! [zy-en zee fair-nōōnftisH]

**don't be angry** seien Sie nicht böse [zy-en zee nisHt bur-zuh]

**beach** der Strand [shtrant]
  **on the beach** am Strand
**beans** die Bohnen [bo-nen]
**beautiful** schön [shurn]
  **that was a beautiful meal** das Essen war
  ausgezeichnet [...var owss-gheh-tsysHnet]
**because** weil [vile]
  **because of the weather** wegen des Wetters
  [vay-ghen...]
**bed** ein Bett
  **a single bed** ein Einzelbett [...ine-tsel-bet...]
  **a double bed** ein Doppelbett
  **I'm off to bed** ich geh' ins Bett [isH gay inss...]
  **you haven't changed my bed** Sie haben die
  Bettwäsche nicht gewechselt [zee hah-ben dee
  bet-vesh-uh nisHt geveksselt]
**bed and breakfast** Zimmer mit Frühstück
  [tsimmer mit frōō-shtōck]

> ✈ Look for the sign **Zimmer frei**, if you want
> to stay in a private house. But these tend
> to be in rural areas only. You could also
> try a **Frühstückspension** or **Gasthaus** for
> simpler accommodation.

**bedroom** das Schlafzimmer [shlahf-tsimmer]
**bee** eine Biene [been-uh]
**beef** das Rindfleisch [rint-flysh]
**beer** ein Bier [beer]
  **two beers, please** zwei Bier, bitte [tsvy beer
  bittuh]

> ✈ Ask for **ein großes Bier** [ine grohs-ess beer]
> 'a large beer' or **ein kleines Beer** [...kline-
> ess...] 'a small beer'.
> **Eine Maß** [ine-uh mahss] is a typical
> Bavarian measure: a litre of beer.
> **Pils** is the most lager-like beer. Other

kinds you could try are **Weizen** (made with wheat, mainly Bavarian but served all over Germany), **Kölsch** (a Cologne speciality), **Alt** (a dark beer found mainly in the Rhine area) or **Berliner Weiße**, which is **Weizenbier** with raspberry or other flavouring.

**before: before breakfast** vor dem Frühstück [for daym frōo-shtōock]

**before we leave** bevor wir gehen [buh-for veer gay-en]

**I haven't been here before** ich bin hier noch nie gewesen [isH bin heer noKH nee gheh-vay-zen]

**begin: when does it begin?** wann fängt es an? [van fengt...]

**beginner** der Anfänger [an-fenger]

*(woman)* die Anfängerin

**behind** hinten

**the car behind me** das Auto hinter mir

**Belgium** Belgien [bel-ghee-un]

**believe: I don't believe you** das glaub' ich Ihnen nicht [dass glowp isH ee-nen nisHt ]

**I believe you** ich glaube Ihnen [isH glow-buh ee-nen]

**bell** *(in hotel, on door)* die Klingel

*(of church etc)* die Glocke

**belong: that belongs to me** das gehört mir [dass gheh-hurt meer]

**who does this belong to?** wem gehört das? [vaym...]

**below** unten [ōonten]

**below the knee** unterhalb des Knies [ōonterhalp...]

**belt** der Gürtel [gōortel]

**bend** *(in road)* die Kurve [koor-vuh]

**berries** die Beeren [bay-ren]

**berth** *(on ship)* das Bett
**besetzt** engaged; full
**beside** neben [nay-ben]
**best** beste [best-uh]
  **it's the best holiday I've ever had** das ist der schönste Urlaub meines Lebens [shurn-stuh oor-lowp mine-ess lay-benz]
**Betreten des Rasens verboten** keep off the grass
**Betreten verboten** keep out
**better** besser
  **haven't you got anything better?** haben Sie nichts Besseres? [hah-ben zee nisHts...]
  **are you feeling better?** geht es Ihnen besser? [gayt ess ee-nen...]
  **I'm feeling a lot better** es geht mir viel besser [ess gayt meer feel...]
**between** zwischen [tsvishen]
**bewachter Parkplatz** supervised car park
**beyond** jenseits [yayn-zites]
**bicycle** ein Fahrrad [far-raht]
**big** groß [grohss]
  **a big one** ein großer [ine grohss-ser]
  **that's too big** das ist zu groß [dass ist tsoo...]
  **have you got a bigger one?** haben Sie nichts Größeres? [hah-ben zee nisHts grurss-er-ess]
**bike** das Rad [raht]
**bikini** ein Bikini
**bill** die Rechnung [resH-noong]
  **could I have the bill, please?** zahlen, bitte [tsah-len bittuh]
**bird** der Vogel [fo-ghel]
**birthday** der Geburtstag [gheh-boorts-tahg]
  **happy birthday!** herzlichen Glückwunsch (zum Geburtstag)! [hairts-lisHen glook-voonsh (tsoom gheh-boorts-tahg)]
  **it's my birthday** ich habe Geburtstag

**biscuit** ein Keks
**bit: just a little bit for me** nur ein bisschen für
mich [noor ine bis-sHen fōōr misH]
  **that's a bit too expensive** das ist ein bisschen
  zu teuer [...tsoo toy-er]
  **a bit of that cake** ein *Stückchen* von dem
  Kuchen da [ine shtōōck-sHen fon daym kooKHen]
  **a big bit** ein großes Stück [...shtōōck]
**bitte eintreten** please enter
**bitte klingeln** please ring
**bitte klopfen** please knock
**bitte nicht stören** please do not disturb
**bitter** *(taste)* bitter
  *(apple)* sauer [zow-er]
**black** schwarz [shvarts]
**blackout: he's had a blackout** er ist ohnmächtig
geworden [air ist ohn-mesH-tisH gheh-vorden]
**blanket** die Decke [deck-uh]
**bleach** *(for cleaning)* das Bleichmittel [blysH-]
**bleed** bluten [blooten]
**bless you!** *(after sneeze)* Gesundheit! [gheh-zōōnt-
hite]
**blind** *(cannot see)* blind [blint]
**blinds** das Rollo
**blister** eine Blase [blah-zuh]
**blocked** *(pipe)* verstopft [fair-shtopft]
  *(road)* blockiert [blockeert]
**blonde** eine Blondine [blond-ee-nuh]
**blood** das Blut [bloot]
  **his blood group is...** er hat Blutgruppe... [air
  hat bloot-grōōp-uh]
  **I've got high blood pressure** ich habe hohen
  Blutdruck [isH hah-buh ho-en bloot-drōōck]
  **he needs a blood transfusion** er braucht eine
  Bluttransfusion [air browKHt ine-uh bloot-tranz-
  fooz-ee-ohn]
**bloody: that's bloody good!** das ist verdammt

gut! [fair-damt goot]
**bloody hell!** *(annoyed)* verdammt nochmal!
[...noKHmahl]
*(amazed)* Wahnsinn! [vahn-zin]
**blouse** die Bluse [bloo-zuh]
**blue** blau [blow]
**board: full board** Vollpension [fol-penz-ee-ohn]
  **half board** Halbpension [halp-]
**boarding pass** die Bordkarte [bort-kartuh]
**boat** das Boot [boht]
  *(bigger)* das Schiff [shif]
**body** der Körper [kurper]
  *(corpse)* eine Leiche [lysH-uh]
**boiled egg** ein gekochtes Ei [gheh-koKH-tess I]
**bolt** der Riegel [reeghel]
**bone** der Knochen [kuh-noKHen]
  *(in fish)* die Gräte [grayt-uh]
**bonnet** *(of car)* die Motorhaube [mo-tor-how-buh]
**book** das Buch [booKH]
  **can I book a seat for...?** kann ich einen Platz
  für...reservieren lassen? [...ine-en...fŏŏr...
  rezairveeren...]
  **I'd like to book a table for two** ich möchte
  gerne einen Tisch für zwei Personen reservieren
  [isH mursHtuh gairn-uh ine-en tish...]

> *YOU MAY THEN HEAR*
> für welche Uhrzeit? *for what time?*
> auf welchen Namen? *and the name is?*

**booking office** die Kasse [kassuh]
**bookshop** eine Buchhandlung [booKH-hantlŏŏng]
**boot** der Stiefel [shteefel]
  *(of car)* der Kofferraum [koffer-rowm]
**booze: I had too much booze last night** ich
  habe gestern Abend zu viel getrunken [isH hah-
  buh ghestern ah-bent tsoo feel gheh-trŏŏnken]
**border** die Grenze [grents-uh]

**bored: I'm bored** mir ist langweilig [meer ist lang-vile-isH]

**boring** langweilig [lang-vile-isH]

**born: I was born in...** ich bin in...geboren [isH bin in...gheh-bor-ren]

**borrow: can I borrow...?** leihst du mir...? [lyst doo meer...]

**boss** der Chef [shef]
*(woman)* die Chefin

**both** beide [by-duh]
**I'll take both of them** ich nehme beide [isH nay-muh...]

**bottle** die Flasche [flash-uh]

> ✈ There's a **Flaschenpfand** on glass and plastic bottles: take your bottles back to any shop that sells them and you'll get a refund.

**bottle-opener** der Flaschenöffner [flashen-urfner]

**bottom** *(of person)* der Po
**at the bottom of the mountain** am Fuß des Berges [am fooss...]

**bouncer** der Rausschmeißer [rowss-shmysser]

**bowl** *(for soup etc)* die Schüssel [shoossel]

**box** die Schachtel [shahKH-tel]
*(wooden)* die Kiste [kistuh]

**boy** ein Junge [yoong-uh]

**boyfriend** der Freund [froynt]

**bra** der BH [bay-hah]

**bracelet** das Armband [arm-bant]

**brake** die Bremse [brem-zuh]
**could you check the brakes?** könnten Sie die Bremsen nachsehen? [kurnten zee dee brem-zen nahKH-zay-en]
**I had to brake suddenly** ich musste plötzlich bremsen [isH moostuh plurts-lisH brem-zen]
**he didn't brake** er hat nicht gebremst [air hat

nisHt gheh-bremst]

**brandy** der Weinbrand [vine-brant]

**bread** das Brot [broht]

**could we have some bread and butter?**
könnten wir etwas Brot und Butter haben?
[kurnten veer etvass broht oont booter hah-ben]

**some more bread, please** noch etwas Brot,
bitte [noкн etvass broht bittuh]

> ✈ There's a wide range of types of bread in
> Germany. Try **Roggenbrot** (rye bread),
> **Sonnenblumenbrot** (with sunflower
> seeds) or **Pumpernickel** (dense and black).

**break** *(verb)* brechen [bresHen]

**I think I've broken my arm** ich glaube, ich
habe mir den Arm gebrochen [...glowbuh isH
hah-buh meer...gheh-broкнen]

**you've broken it** Sie haben es kaputt gemacht
[zee hah-ben ess...gheh-maкнt]

**break into: my room has been broken into**
man hat in mein Zimmer eingebrochen [...mine
tsimmer ine-gheh-broкнen]

**my car has been broken into** man hat meinen
Wagen aufgebrochen [...mine-en vah-ghen owf-
gheh-broкнen]

**breakable** zerbrechlich [tsair-bresHlisH]

**breakdown** die Panne [pan-uh]

**I've had a breakdown** ich hatte eine Panne

**a nervous breakdown** ein Nerven-
zusammenbruch [nair-ven tsoo-sammen-brooкн]

**breakfast** das Frühstück [froo-shtöock]

**breast** die Brust [broost]

**breathe** atmen [aht-men]

**I can't breathe** ich bekomme keine Luft [isH
buh-kommuh kine-uh looft]

**bridge** die Brücke [broockuh]

**briefcase** die Aktenmappe [akten-mapuh]

**brighten up: do you think it'll brighten up later?** glauben Sie, es *klärt* sich später *auf*? [glow-ben zee ess klairt ziSH shpayter owf]

**brilliant** großartig [grohss-artiSH]
*(swimmer, driver etc)* ausgezeichnet [owss-gheh-tsySH-net]
**brilliant!** toll!

**bring** bringen
**could you bring it to my hotel?** könnten Sie es mir ins Hotel bringen? [kurnten zee ess meer inss...]

**Britain** Großbritannien [grohss-britahn-ee-un]

**British** britisch [breetish]
**the British** die Briten [breeten]
**I'm British** ich bin Brite [breetuh]
*(woman)* ich bin Britin [breetin]

**brochure** der Prospekt
**have you got any brochures about...?** haben Sie Prospekte über...? [hah-ben zee...ööber]

**broken** kaputt

**brooch** die Brosche [bro-shuh]

**brother: my brother** mein Bruder [mine brooder]

**brown** braun [brown]

**browse: can I just browse around?** kann ich mich mal umsehen? [kann iSH miSH oom-zay-en]

**bruise** ein blauer Fleck [ine blow-er...]

**brunette** eine Brünette [bröö-nettuh]

**brush** die Bürste [böörstuh]
*(painter's)* der Pinsel

**bucket** der Eimer [I-mer]

**buffet** das Büfett [bööf-ay]

**building** das Gebäude [gheh-boy-duh]
*(residential)* das Haus [howss]

**bulb** die (Glüh)birne [(glöö)beern-uh]
**the bulb's gone** die Birne ist durchgebrannt [...doorSH-gheh-brant]

**bumbag** eine Gürteltasche [göörtel-tash-uh]

**bump: he's had a bump on the head** er hat sich den Kopf angeschlagen [air hat zisH dayn kopf an-gheh-shlah-ghen]

**bumper** die Stoßstange [shtohss-shtang-uh]

**bunch of flowers** ein Blumenstrauß [bloomen-shtrowss]

**bunk** das Bett
*(on ship)* die Koje [ko-yuh]

**bunk beds** ein Etagenbett [aytah-Jen-]

**bureau de change** die Wechselstube [veksel-shtoobuh]

**burglar** ein Einbrecher [ine-bresHer]
*(woman)* eine Einbrecherin

**burgle: our flat's been burgled** bei uns ist eingebrochen worden [by conss ist ine-gheh-broKHen vorden]

---

**they've taken all my money** man hat mir mein ganzes Geld gestohlen [...meer mine gants-ess ghelt gheh-shtohlen]

---

**burn: this meat is burnt** das Fleisch ist verbrannt [...flysh ist fair-brant]

**my arms are burnt** ich habe einen Sonnenbrand an den Armen [isH hah-buh ine-en zonnen-brant...]

**can you give me something for these burns?** können Sie mir etwas für diese Brandwunden geben? [kurnen zee meer etvass foor deez-uh brannt-voonden gay-ben]

**bus** der Bus [booss]

**which bus is it for...?** welcher Bus fährt nach...? [velsHer...fairt nahKH]

---

**could you tell me when we get there?** könnten Sie mir sagen, wo ich aussteigen muss? [kurnten zee meer zah-ghen vo isH owss-shty-ghen mooss]

---

✈ It's usually possible to buy tickets on the bus as well as from the ticket machine at the bus stop. You may have to punch your ticket in the machine on the bus.

**bus station** der Busbahnhof [boossbahn-hohff]
**bus stop** die Bushaltestelle [booss-halt-uh-shtel-uh]
**business: I'm here on business** ich bin geschäftlich hier [isн bin geh-sheft-lisн heer]
**none of your business!** das geht Sie nichts an! [dass gayt zee nisнts an]
**business trip** eine Geschäftsreise [geh-shefts-ry-zuh]
**bust** die Büste
**busy** (streets etc) belebt [buh-laypt]
  (telephone) besetzt
  **are you busy?** haben Sie viel zu tun? [hah-ben zee feel tsoo toon]
  **it's very busy here** es ist sehr viel los hier […zair feel lohss…]
**but** aber [ah-ber]
  **not…but…** nicht…sondern [nisнt…zondern]
**butcher's** der Fleischer [flysher]
**butter** die Butter [booter]
**button** der Knopf [kuh-nopf]
**buy: where can I buy…?** wo kann ich…kaufen? [vo…kowfen]
**by: I'm here by myself** ich bin *allein* hier [isн bin al-ine heer]
  **can you do it by tomorrow?** können Sie es bis morgen erledigen? [kurnen zee ess biss…airlayd-i-ghen]
  **by train/plane** per Zug/Flugzeug [pair…]
  **I parked by the trees** ich habe bei den Bäumen geparkt [isн hah-buh by dayn boy-men geh-parkt]
  **a book by…** ein Buch von… […fon]

# C [tsay]

**cabbage** der Kohl
**cabin** *(on ship)* die Kabine [kabeen-uh]
**cable** *(electric)* das Kabel [kah-bel]
**café** ein Café [kafay]

> ✈ A **Café** will serve mostly coffee and cakes, although alcohol and snacks are served too; for a fuller café-type meal go to a **Gasthaus**.

**cake** der Kuchen [kookhen]
**calculator** der Taschenrechner [tashen-reshner]
**call: will you call the manager?** rufen Sie den Geschäftsführer, bitte! [roofen zee dayn ghehshefts-föörer bittuh]
    **what is this called?** wie nennt man das? [vee...]
    **I'll call back later** *(on phone)* ich rufe später noch einmal an [ish roof-uh shpayter nokh inemal an]
**call box** eine Telefonzelle [telefohn-tselluh]
**calm** ruhig [roo-ish]
    **calm down!** beruhigen Sie sich! [buh-roo-igen zee zish]
**camcorder** ein Camcorder
**camera** die Kamera
**camp: can we camp here?** können wir hier zelten? [kurnen veer heer tselten]
    **a camping holiday** ein Camping-Urlaub [...oor-lowp]
**campsite** der Campingplatz

> ✈ Off-site camping requires the permission of the land-owner and/or the local police.

**can¹: a can of beer** eine *Dose* Bier [ine-uh dohzuh beer]

✈ There is a **Dosenpfand** on cans: take your can back to the stockist and you'll get some money back.

**can²: can I have…?** kann ich…haben? [kan isн hah-ben]

**can you show me…?** können Sie mir…zeigen? [kurnen zee…]

*(familiar)* kannst du mir zeigen…?

**I can't…** ich kann nicht… […nisнт…]

**he/she can't…** er/sie kann nicht… [air/zee…]

**we can't…** wir können nicht… [veer…]

**they can't…** sie können nicht…

**Canada** Kanada

**cancel: I want to cancel my booking** ich möchte meine Buchung *rückgängig machen* [isн mursнtuh mine-uh booкн-∞ong rook-geng-isн mahкнen]

**can we cancel dinner for tonight?** können wir das Abendessen für heute Abend *abbestellen*? [kurnen veer dass ah-bent-essen foor hoytuh ap-buh-shtellen]

**candle** die Kerze [kairts-uh]

**can-opener** ein Dosenöffner [dohzen-urfner]

**capsize** kentern

**car** das Auto, der Wagen [owto, vah-ghen]

**by car** mit dem Auto […daym…]

**carafe** die Karaffe [kar-afuh]

**caravan** der Wohnwagen [vohn-vah-ghen]

**carburettor** der Vergaser [fair-gah-zer]

**cards** die Karten [kairten]

**do you play cards?** spielen Sie Karten? [shpee-len zee…]

**care: goodbye, take care** tschüs, mach's gut [tch∞ss mahкнs goot]

**careful: be careful** seien Sie vorsichtig [zy-en zee for-zisн-tisн]

**car-ferry** die Autofähre [owto-fair-uh]
**car park** der Parkplatz
  *(multistorey)* das Parkhaus [-howss]
**carpet** der Teppich [tepisH]
  *(wall to wall)* der Teppichboden [-bo-den]
**carrier bag** eine Tragetasche [trahg-uh-tash-uh]
**carrot** eine Karotte [karot-uh]
**carry** tragen [trah-ghen]
**carving** die Schnitzerei [shnits-er-ɪ]
**case** *(suitcase)* der Koffer
**cash** das Bargeld [bar-ghelt]
  **I haven't any cash** ich habe kein Bargeld [isH
  hah-buh kine…]
  **will you cash a cheque for me?** können Sie
  mir einen Scheck einlösen? [kurnen zee meer
  ine-en sheck ine-lurzen]
  **I'll pay cash** ich zahle in bar [isH tsahluh…]
**cash desk** die Kasse [kassuh]
**casino** das Kasino
**cassette** die Kassette [kassetuh]
**cassette player** ein Kassettenrekorder
**castle** das Schloss [shloss]
  *(fortress)* die Burg [boorg]
**cat** eine Katze [kats-uh]
**catch: where do we catch the bus?** wo fährt
  der Bus ab? [vo fairt booss ap]
  **he's caught a bug** er hat sich irgendwo
  angesteckt [air hat zisH eergent-vo an-gheh-
  shteckt]
**cathedral** die Kathedrale [katay-drahl-uh]
**catholic** katholisch [kato-lish]
**cave** die Höhle [hur-luh]
**CD** eine CD [tsay-day]
**CD-player** ein CD-Spieler [tsay-day-shpeeler]
**ceiling** die Decke [deck-uh]
**cellophane** das Cellophan [tselo-fahn]
**cent** der Cent

**centigrade** Celsius [tsel-zee-ooss]

> ✈ $C/5 \times 9 + 32 = F$
>
> | centigrade | -5 | 0 | 10 | 15 | 21 | 30 | 36.9 |
> |---|---|---|---|---|---|---|---|
> | Fahrenheit | 23 | 32 | 50 | 59 | 70 | 86 | 98.4 |

**centimetre** ein Zentimeter [tsentee-mayter]

> ✈ 1 cm = 0.39 inches

**central** zentral [tsen-trahl]
  **with central heating** mit Zentralheizung [mit tsen-trahl-hitesoong]
**centre** das Zentrum [tsen-troom]
  **how do we get to the centre?** wie kommen wir zur Stadtmitte? [vee kommen veer tsoor shtat-mit-uh]
**certain** bestimmt [buh-shtimt]
  **are you certain?** sind Sie sicher? [zint zee zisher]
**certificate** eine Bescheinigung [buh-shine-igoong]
**chain** die Kette [ketuh]
**chair** der Stuhl [shtool]
  *(armchair)* der Sessel [zessel]
**chairlift** der Sessellift
**chambermaid** das Zimmermädchen [tsimmer-mayd-shen]
**champagne** der Sekt [zekt]
**change: could you change this into euros?** könnten Sie das in Euro *umtauschen*? [kurnten zee dass in oyro oom-tow-shen]
  **I haven't any change** ich habe kein Kleingeld [ish hah-buh kine kline-ghelt]
  **do you have change for 100 euros?** können Sie auf 100 Euro herausgeben? [...hairowss-gayben]
  **do we have to change trains?** müssen wir *umsteigen*? [moossen veer oom-shty-ghen]
  **I'd like to change my flight** ich möchte

*umbuchen* [ishmursHtuh oom-bookHen]
**I'll just get changed** ich ziehe mich mal um
[ish tsee-uh mish mal oom]
**channel: the Channel** der Ärmelkanal [airmel-kanahl]
**Channel Tunnel** der Kanaltunnel [kanahl-toonel]
**charge: what will you charge?** was verlangen
Sie? [vass fair-langen zee]
**who's in charge?** wer hat hier die
Verantwortung? [vair hat heer dee fair-ant-vort-oong]
**cheap** billig [billisH]
**have you got something cheaper?** haben Sie
etwas Billigeres? [...etvass billig-er-ess]
**cheat: I've been cheated** ich bin betrogen
worden [ish bin buh-tro-ghen vorden]
**check: will you check?** *sehen Sie bitte nach* [zay-en zee bittuh nahkH]
**I've checked** ich habe nachgeprüft [ish hah-buh
nahkH-gheh-prooft]
**we checked in** *(at hotel)* wir haben eingecheckt
[veer hah-ben ine-gheh-checkt]
**we checked out** *(from hotel)* wir haben
ausgecheckt [...owss-]
**check-in desk** der Check-in-Schalter
**check-in time** Check-in
**cheek** *(of face)* die Backe [back-uh]
**cheeky** frech [fresH]
**cheerio** Wiedersehen, tschüs [veeder-zay-en,
tchōōss]
**cheers** *(toast)* Prost! [prohst]
*(thanks)* vielen Dank [feelen...]
**cheese** der Käse [kay-zuh]
**cheeseburger** ein Cheeseburger
**chef** der Koch [kokH]
**chemist's** die Drogerie [drohg-eree]
*(dispensing)* die Apotheke [apo-tay-kuh]

✈ Dispensing chemists display a notice about night service (**Nachtdienst**) and Sunday service (**Sonntagsdienst**).

**cheque** der Scheck [sheck]
  **will you take a cheque?** nehmen Sie Schecks? [nay-men zee shecks]
**cheque book** das Scheckbuch [sheck-bookH]
**cheque card** die Scheckkarte [sheck-kartuh]
**chest** die Brust [brœst]
**chewing gum** der Kaugummi [kow-gœmee]
**chicken** das Hähnchen [hayn-sHen]
**chickenpox** die Windpocken [vintpocken]
**child** ein Kind [kint]
**child minder** eine Tagesmutter [tahgess-mœoter]
**children** die Kinder [kinnder]
  **a children's portion** ein Kinderteller

✈ There is no law against taking children into a pub.

**chin** das Kinn
**china** das Porzellan [ports-elahn]
**chips** die Pommes frites [pom frit]
  *(in casino)* die Chips
**chocolate** die Schokolade [shok-o-lahduh]
  **a hot chocolate** eine heiße Schokolade [hyssuh...]
  **a box of chocolates** eine Schachtel Pralinen [ine-uh shahkH-tel pra-leenen]
**chop: pork/lamb chop** Schweine-/Lamm-kotelett
**Christian name** der Vorname [for-nah-muh]
**Christmas** Weihnachten [vy-nahkH-ten]
  **on Christmas Eve** am Heiligabend [hile-isH-ah-bent]
  **Happy Christmas** fröhliche Weihnachten [frurlisH-uh...]

✈ Christmas in Germany starts on the 24th (**Heiligabend**) when work normally stops at midday; presents are given on the evening of the 24th; holidays on Christmas Day (**der erste Weihnachtstag**) and Boxing Day (**der zweite Weihnachtstag**); on December 6th children traditionally find sweets and nuts put in their shoes during the night by **der Nikolaus**.

**church** die Kirche [keersʜuh]
**cider** ein Apfelmost
**cigar** die Zigarre [tsigaruh]
**cigarette** die Zigarette [tsigaretuh]
**cinema** das Kino [keeno]

✈ Many cinemas offer reduced prices once a week; this **Kinotag** is usually a Tuesday.

**circle** der Kreis [krice]
 *(in cinema)* der Rang
**city** die Stadt [shtat]
**city centre** die Stadtmitte [shtat-mit-uh]
**claim** *(insurance)* der Anspruch [an-shprooκʜ]
**clarify** klären [klairen]
**clean** *(adjective)* sauber [zowber]
  **it's not clean** das ist nicht sauber
  **my room hasn't been cleaned today** in meinem Zimmer ist heute nicht sauber gemacht worden [in mine-em tsimmer ist hoytuh nisʜt zowber gheh-maʜκʜt vorden]
**cleansing cream** die Reinigungscreme [rine-igoongs-kray-muh]
**clear: I'm not clear about it** ich bin mir darüber nicht im Klaren [isʜ bin meer darㄧober nisʜt im klah-ren]
**clever** klug [kloog]
 *(skilful)* geschickt [gheh-shickt]

**climate** das Klima [kleema]

**climb: we're going to climb...** wir besteigen... [veer buh-shty-ghen...]

**climber** ein Bergsteiger [bairk-shty-gher]
*(woman)* eine Bergsteigerin

**climbing boots** die Bergstiefel [bairk-shteefel]

**clip** *(ski)* die Schnalle [shnaluh]

**cloakroom** *(for clothes)* die Garderobe [garduh-ro-buh]

**clock** die Uhr [oor]

**close¹** nahe [nah-uh]
*(weather)* schwül [shvool]
**is it close?** ist es in der Nähe? [...dair nay-uh...]

**close²: when do you close?** wann *machen* Sie *zu*? [van maHKHen zee tsoo]

**closed** geschlossen [gheh-shlossen]

**cloth** das Tuch [tooKH]
*(rag)* der Lappen

**clothes** die Kleidung [klydoong]

**clothes peg** eine Wäscheklammer [vesh-uh-]

**cloud** die Wolke [volk-uh]

**clubbing: we're going clubbing** wir gehen clubbing [veer gay-en...]

**clutch** die Kupplung [koop-loong]
**the clutch is slipping** die Kupplung schleift [...shlyft]

**coach** der (Reise)bus [(ry-zuh)booss]

**coach party** die Reisegesellschaft [ry-zuh-gheh-zel-shafft]

**coach trip** eine Busreise [booss-ry-zuh]

**coast** die Küste [koostuh]
**at the coast** an der Küste

**coastguard** die Küstenwache [koosten-vahKH-uh]

**coat** der Mantel

**cockroach** eine Küchenschabe [kooKHen-sha-buh]

**coffee** ein Kaffee [kafay]
**a white coffee** ein Milchkaffee [milsH-kafay]

**a black coffee** ein Kaffee

✈ Coffee is normally served black with cream or milk separate. **Mokka** is a very strong coffee.

---

*YOU MAY HEAR*
Kännchen oder Tasse? *pot or cup?*

---

**coke®** eine Cola
**cold** kalt
**I'm cold** ich friere [isH free-ruh]
**I've got a cold** ich habe eine Erkältung [isH hah-buh ine-uh airkel-tœong]
**collapse: he's collapsed** er ist zusammengebrochen [air ist tsoo-tsammen-gheh-broкHen]
**collar** der Kragen [krah-ghen]

| ✈ UK: | 14 | 14.5 | 15 | 15.5 | 16 | 16.5 | 17 |
|---|---|---|---|---|---|---|---|
| Germany: | 36 | 37 | 38 | 39 | 41 | 42 | 43 |

**collect: I've come to collect...** ich möchte ...abholen [isH mursHtuh...ap-hohl-en]
**colour** die Farbe [far-buh]
**have you any other colours?** haben Sie noch andere Farben? [hah-ben zee noкH ander-uh far-ben]
**comb** ein Kamm
**come** kommen
**I come from London** ich komme aus London [isH kommuh owss...]
**when is he coming?** wann kommt er? [van komt air]
**we came here yesterday** wir sind gestern hier angekommen [veer zint ghestern heer an-gheh-kommen]
**come with me** kommen Sie mit! [...zee...]
**come here** kommen Sie her! [...hair]

**come on!** komm schon! [...shohn]

**oh, come on!** *(disbelief)* ach was! [ahкн vass]

**comfortable** bequem [buh-kvaym]

**company** *(business)* das Unternehmen [connternaymen]

   **you're good company** ich bin gern mit Ihnen zusammen [isн bin gairn mit ee-nen tsoo-zammen]

**compartment** *(in train)* das Abteil [ap-tile]

**compass** der Kompass [kompas]

**compensation** die Entschädigung [ent-shayd-igoong]

   **I want compensation** ich verlange Schadenersatz [isн fair-lang-uh shahden-airzats]

**complain** sich beschweren [zisн buh-shvairen]

   **I want to complain about my room** ich möchte mich über mein Zimmer beschweren [isн mursнtuh misн ōōber...]

**completely** völlig [furlisн]

**complicated: it's very complicated** es ist sehr kompliziert [...zair komplits-eert]

**compliment: my compliments to the chef** Kompliment an den Koch [...dayn koкн]

**compulsory: is it compulsory?** ist es Pflicht? [...pflisнt]

**computer** ein 'Computer'

**concert** das Konzert [kontsairt]

**concussion** eine Gehirnerschütterung [gheh-heern-air-shōōt-eroong]

**condition** *(term)* die Bedingung [buh-ding-oong]

   **it's not in very good condition** es ist nicht in besonders gutem Zustand [...nisнt in buh-zonders gootem tsoo-shtant]

**condom** ein Kondom [kon-dohm]

**conference** die Konferenz [kon-fer-ents]

**confirm** bestätigen [buh-shtayt-ighen]

**confuse: you're confusing me** Sie bringen mich

durcheinander [zee bringen misH doorsH-ine-ander]

**congratulations!** herzlichen Glückwunsch! [hairts-lisHen glœck-voonsh]

**conjunctivitis** die Bindehautentzündung [binduh-howt-ent-tsœn-doong]

**conman** der Schwindler [shvintler]

**connection** die Verbindung [fair-bindoong]

**connoisseur** der Kenner
*(woman)* die Kennerin

**conscious** bewusst [buh-voost]

**consciousness: he's lost consciousness** er ist bewusstlos [air ist buh-voost-lohss]

**constipation** die Verstopfung [fair-shtopf-oong]

**consul** der Konsul [kon-zool]
*(woman)* die Konsulin

**consulate** das Konsulat [kon-zool-aht]

**contact: how can I contact…?** wie kann ich… erreichen? [vee kann isH…air-rysHen]

**contact lenses** die Kontaktlinsen [-zen]

**convenient** günstig [gœnstisH]

**cook: it's not cooked** es ist nicht gar
**you're a good cook** Sie kochen ausgezeichnet [zee kokHen owss-gheh-tsysH-net]

**cooker** der Herd [hairt]

**cool** kühl [kœl]
*(great)* cool

**corkscrew** der Korkenzieher [korken-tsee-er]

**corner** die Ecke [eck-uh]
**can we have a corner table?** können wir einen Ecktisch haben? [kurnen veer ine-en eck-tish hah-ben]
**on the corner** an der Ecke
**in the corner** in der Ecke

**cornflakes** die 'Cornflakes'

**correct** richtig [risH-tisH]

**cosmetics** die Kosmetika [kosmaytika]

**cost: what does it cost?** was kostet das? [vass kostet dass]

> **that's too much** das ist zu viel [dass ist tsoofeel]
> **I'll take it** ich nehme es [ish nay-muh ess]

**cot** ein Kinderbett [kinnder-]
**cotton** die Baumwolle [bowm-voluh]
**cotton wool** die Watte [vatuh]
**couchette** der Liegesitz [leeg-uh-zits]
**cough** der Husten [hoosten]
**cough drops** die Hustentropfen
**could: could you please...?** könnten Sie, bitte,...? [kurnten zee bittuh]
**could I have...?** könnte ich...haben? [kurntuh ish...hah-ben]
**we couldn't...** wir konnten nicht... [veer...]
**country** das Land [lant]
**in the country(side)** auf dem Land [owf daym...]
**couple: a couple of...** ein paar... [ine par]
**courier** der Reiseleiter [ry-zuh-ly-ter]
*(woman)* die Reiseleiterin
**course: of course** natürlich [natoor-lish]
**court: I'll take you to court** ich werde Sie vor Gericht bringen [ish vair-duh zee for gheh-risht...]
**cousin: my cousin** *(male)* mein Cousin [koo-zan]
*(female)* meine Kusine [koo-zeen-uh]
**cover: keep him covered** decken Sie ihn zu [...zee een tsoo]
**cover charge** das Gedeck [gheh-deck]
**cow** die Kuh [koo]
**crab** die Krabbe [krabuh]
**craftshop** das Kunsthandwerkgeschäft [koonst-hant-vairk-gheh-sheft]
**crap: this is crap** das ist Mist

**crash: there's been a crash** da ist ein *Unfall*
   passiert [...ine con-fal pas-eert]
**crash helmet** der Sturzhelm [shtoorts-helm]
**crazy** verrückt [fair-rœckt]
   **you're crazy** du spinnst [doo shpinst]
   **that's crazy** das ist verrückt
**cream** die Sahne [zah-nuh]
   *(with butter, for skin)* die Creme [kraym]
**credit card** die Kreditkarte [kredeet-kartuh]
**crisps** die Chips
**cross** *(verb)* gehen über [gay-en ööber]
**crossroads** die Kreuzung [kroytsoong]
**crowded** überfüllt [ööber-fœlt]
   **it's crowded** es ist sehr voll [...zair fol]
**cruise** die Bootsfahrt [bohts-fart]
**crutch** *(for invalid)* die Krücke [krœck-uh]
**cry: don't cry** weinen Sie nicht [vine-en zee
   nisHt]
**cup** die Tasse [tass-uh]
   **a cup of coffee** eine Tasse Kaffee [ine-uh...
   kaffay]
**cupboard** der Schrank [shrank]
**curry** der Curry
**curtains** der Vorhang [for-hang]
**cushion** das Kissen
**Customs** der Zoll [tsol]
**cut** *(verb)* schneiden [shny-den]
   **I've cut myself** ich habe mich geschnitten [isH
   hah-buh misH gheh-shnitten]
**cycle: can we cycle there?** können wir mit dem
   Rad dorthin fahren? [kurnen veer mit daym raht
   dort-hin faren]
**cyclist** der Radfahrer [raht-farer]
   *(female)* die Radfahrerin
**cylinder-head gasket** die Zylinderkopfdichtung
   [tsöölinder-kopf-disH-toong]

# D [day]

**dad: my dad** mein Vater [mine fahter]
**damage: I'll pay for the damage** ich werde für
den *Schaden* aufkommen [ish vair-duh foor dayn
shahden owf-kommen]
**damaged** beschädigt [buh-shaydisht]
**Damen** ladies
**damn!** verdammt! [fair-damt]
**damp** feucht [foysht]
**dance: would you like to dance?** möchten Sie
tanzen? [mursHten zee tantsen]
**dangerous** gefährlich [geh-fair-lish]
**dark** dunkel [doonkel]
   **when does it get dark?** wann wird es dunkel?
   [van veert ess...]
   **dark blue** dunkelblau [doonkel-blow]
**darling** Liebling [leepling]
**date: what's the date?** der Wievielte ist heute?
[dair vee-feel-tuh ist hoytuh]
   **can we make a date?** *(romantic)* sollen wir uns
   mal treffen? [zol-en veer oonss...]

> ✈ To say the date as in 'on the 5th of May'
> in German add letters **-ten** to the number
> if 1-19, and **-sten** if 20-31; see numbers
> on pages 159-160; exceptions: **first** ersten,
> **third** dritten, **seventh** siebten.

---

**in 1982** neunzehnhundertzweiundachtzig
[noyn-tsayn-hoondert-tsvy-oont-aKHt-tsisH]
**in 2004** zweitausendvier [tsvy-towzent-feer]
**on the fifth of May** am fünften Mai [am foonf-
ten my]

---

**dates** *(fruit)* die Datteln
**daughter: my daughter** meine Tochter [mine-uh

toᴋʜter]

**day** der Tag [tahg]
  **the day after** am Tag danach [...danahᴋʜ]
  **the day before** am Tag zuvor [...tsoofor]

**dazzle: his lights were dazzling me** seine
  Scheinwerfer haben mich *geblendet* [zine-uh
  shine-vair-fer hah-ben misʜ gheh-blendet]

**dead** tot [toht]

**deaf** taub [towp]

**deal: it's a deal** abgemacht [ap-gheh-mahᴋʜt]
  **will you deal with it?** kümmern Sie sich bitte
  darum? [kᴓmern zee zisʜ bittuh da-rᴓom]

**dear** *(expensive)* teuer [toyer]
  **Dear Martin** Lieber Martin [leeber...]
  **Dear Kathrin** Liebe Kathrin
  **Dear Mr Kunz** Sehr geehrter Herr Kunz [zair
  gheh-airter...]

**December** Dezember [daytsember]

**deckchair** der Liegestuhl [leeguh-shtool]

**declare: I have nothing to declare** nichts zu
  verzollen [nisʜts tsoo fair-tsollen]

**deep** tief [teef]

**de-icer** der Enteiser [ent-ize-er]

**delay: the flight was delayed** der Flug hatte
  Verspätung [dair floog hat-uh fair-shpay-tᴓong]

**deliberately** absichtlich [ap-zisʜt-lisʜ]

**delicate** *(person)* zart [tsart]

**delicious** köstlich [kurstlisʜ]

**de luxe** Luxus- [lᴓoksᴓoss]

**dent** eine Delle [deluh]

**dentist** der Zahnarzt [tsahn-artst]
  *(woman)* die Zahnärztin [-airts-tin]

> *YOU MAY HEAR*
> welcher Zahn ist es? *which tooth is it?*
> bitte weit öffnen *open wide please*
> bitte ausspülen *rinse out please*

*go to* **doctor**

**dentures** das Gebiss [gheh-biss]
   *(partial)* die Zahnprothese [tsahn-pro-tay-zuh]
**deny: I deny it** das bestreite ich [dass buh-shtry-tuh iSH]
**deodorant** das Deodorant [day-odorant]
**departure** die Abreise [ap-ry-zuh]
   *(of bus,train)* die Abfahrt [ap-fart]
   *(of plane)* der Abflug [ap-floog]
**departure lounge** der Wartebereich [vartuh-buh-rySH]
**depend: it depends** das kommt darauf an
   [...darowf...]
   **it depends on...** das kommt auf...an
**deposit** *(downpayment)* die Anzahlung [an-tsah-loong]
   *(security)* die Kaution [kow-tsee-ohn]
   **do I have to leave a deposit?** muss ich eine
   Kaution hinterlegen? [mooss iSH ine-uh...hinter-lay-ghen]
**depressed** deprimiert [day-primeert]
**depth** die Tiefe [teef-uh]
**desperate: I'm desperate for a drink** ich
   brauche dringend was zu trinken [iSH browKHuh
   dringent...tsoo...]
**dessert** der Nachtisch [nahKH-]
**destination** das Reiseziel [ry-zuh-tseel]
**detergent** das Waschmittel
**detour** der Umweg [oom-vayg]
**develop: could you develop these?** könnten
   Sie diese *entwickeln*? [kurnten zee dee-zuh ent-vickeln]
**diabetic** der Diabetiker [dee-abaytiker]
   *(woman)* die Diabetikerin
**diamond** der Diamant [dee-amant]
**diarrhoea** der Durchfall [doorSH-fal]
   **have you got something for diarrhoea?**

haben Sie ein Mittel gegen Durchfall? [hah-ben
zee...]

**diary** das Tagebuch [tah-gheh-bookH]

**dictionary** ein Wörterbuch [vurter-bookH]

**didn't** *go to* **not**

**die** sterben [shtairben]

**diesel** Diesel

**diet** eine Diät [dee-ayt]

  **I'm on a diet** ich mache eine Schlankheitskur
[isH mahkH-uh ine-uh shlank-hites-koor]

**different: they are different** sie sind verschieden
[zee zint fair-sheeden]

  **can I have a different room?** kann ich ein
anderes Zimmer haben? [...ine an-der-ess...]

**difficult** schwierig [shveerisH]

**dinghy** das Dingi [ding-ee]

  *(rubber)* das Schlauchboot [shlowkH-boht]

**dining room** das Esszimmer [ess-tsimmer]

  *(in hotel)* der Speiseraum [shpy-zuh-rowm]

**dinner** *(evening)* das (Abend)essen [ah-bent-]

**dinner jacket** eine Smokingjacke [-yack-uh]

**direct** *(adjective)* direkt [dee-rekt]

  **does it go direct?** ist es eine Direktverbindung?
[...ine-uh deerekt-fairbindoong]

**dirty** schmutzig [shmootsisH]

**disabled** behindert [buh-hindert]

**disappear** verschwinden [fair-shvinden]

  **it's just disappeared** es ist einfach
verschwunden [ess ist ine-fahkH...]

**disappointing** enttäuschend [ent-toyshent]

**disco** eine Disko

**discount** der Rabatt

  *(for cash)* der Skonto

**disgusting** widerlich [veeder-lisH]

**dish** *(food)* das Gericht [gheh-risHt]

  *(plate)* die Schüssel [shoossel]

**dishonest** unehrlich [oonairlisH]

**disinfectant** das Desinfektionsmittel [days-infek-tsee-ohns-]

**disposable camera** eine Einwegkamera [ine-vayg-]

**distance** die Entfernung [ent-fair-noong]
  **in the distance** in der Ferne [in dair fairnuh]

**distress signal** ein Notsignal [noht-zignahl]

**disturb: the noise is disturbing us** der Lärm
  *stört* uns [dair lairm shturt oonss]

**diving board** das Sprungbrett [shproong-]

**divorced** geschieden [geh-sheeden]

**do** machen [mahkhen]
  **what are you doing tonight?** was machen Sie
  heute Abend? [vass…zee hoytuh ah-bent]
  **how do you do it?** wie macht man das? [vee
  mahkht…]
  **will you do it for me?** machen Sie das für
  mich? […foor mish]
  **I've never done it before** ich habe das noch
  nie gemacht [ish hah-buh dass nokh nee gheh-mahkht]
  **he did it** *(it was him)* er war's [air varss]
  **I was doing 60 (kph)** ich bin mit mit 60kmh
  gefahren [ish bin mit zesh-tsish gheh-faren]
  **how do you do?** guten Tag! [gooten tahg]

**doctor** der Arzt [artst]
  *(woman)* die Ärztin [airts-tin]
  **I need a doctor** ich brauche einen Arzt [ish
  browkhuh ine-en…]

✈ Make sure you get a form E111 from a
UK post office before you leave. If you
need a doctor (or dentist) in Germany,
get in touch with an insurance company
or **Versicherungsgesellschaft**. This
insurance company will give you a list of
contracted-in doctors. You'll then get free

treatment or will be able to get your costs
reimbursed.

---

*YOU MAY HEAR*
haben Sie das schon einmal gehabt? *have
you had this before?*
wo tut es weh? *where does it hurt?*
nehmen Sie zurzeit Medikamente? *are you
taking any medication at the moment?*
nehmen Sie eine davon *take one of these*
dreimal/viermal täglich *three times/four
times a day*

---

**document** das Dokument [-oom<small>e</small>nt]
**dog** ein Hund [h<small>oo</small>nt]
**don't!** nicht! [ni<small>SH</small>t]
*go to* **not**
**door** die Tür [t<small>oo</small>r]
**dosage** die Dosis [d<small>o</small>h-ziss]
**double room** ein Doppelzimmer [d<small>o</small>ppel-
tsimmer]
**double whisky** ein doppelter Whisky
**down: down there** drunten [dr<small>oo</small>nten]
  **get down!** runter! [r<small>oo</small>nter]
  **it's just down the road** es ist nur ein Stückchen
  weiter [...noor ine sht<small>oo</small>ck-<small>SH</small>en vy-ter]
**downstairs** unten [<small>oo</small>nten]
**drain** das (Abfluss)rohr [ap-fl<small>oo</small>ss-ror]
**drawing pin** die Reißzwecke [r<small>i</small>ce-tsveck-uh]
**dress** das Kleid [klite]

| ✈ | | | | | | | |
|---|---|---|---|---|---|---|---|
| UK: | 8 | 10 | 12 | 14 | 16 | 18 | 20 |
| Germany: | 34 | 36 | 38 | 40 | 42 | 44 | 46 |

**dressing** *(for cut)* der Verband [fair-b<small>a</small>nt]
  *(for salad)* die Sauce [z<small>o</small>hsuh]
**drink** *(verb)* trinken
  *(alcoholic)* der Drink

**something to drink** etwas zu trinken [etvass tsoo…]

**would you like a drink?** möchten Sie etwas trinken? [murSHten zee…]

**I don't drink** ich trinke keinen Alkohol [iSH trinkuh kine-en alkohohl]

✈ Licensing hours are very relaxed in Germany.

**drinkable: is the water drinkable?** kann man das Wasser trinken?

**drive** fahren [faren]

**I've been driving all day** ich bin den ganzen Tag gefahren [iSH…gantsen tahg gheh-faren]

✈ Children up to the age of 12 (or a height of 1.5m) have to sit in special child seats. Seat belts, red triangle and first aid kit compulsory; *go to* **speed**.

**driver** der Fahrer
*(woman)* die Fahrerin

**driving licence** der Führerschein [fœrer-shine]

**drown: he's drowning** er ertrinkt! [air airtrinkt]

**drücken** push

**drug** das Medikament
*(narcotic etc)* die Droge [dro-guh]

**drug dealer** ein Dealer
*(woman)* eine Dealerin

**drunk** *(adjective)* betrunken [buh-troonken]

**dry** *(adjective)* trocken

**dry-clean** chemisch reinigen [kaymish ry-nigen]

**dry-cleaner's** die Reinigung [ry-nigoong]

**due: when is the bus due?** wann soll der Bus ankommen? [van zol dair booss…]

**Durchfahrt verboten** no through road

**Durchgangsverkehr** through traffic

**during** während [vair-rent]

**Duschen** showers
**dust** der Staub [shtowp]
**duty-free shop** der 'Duty-free-Shop'
**DVD** eine DVD [day-fow-day]

# E [ay]

**each: can we have one each?** können wir
*jeder* eins haben? [kurnen veer yay-der ine-ss
hah-ben]
  **how much are they each?** was kosten sie pro
Stück? [vass kosten zee pro shtöock]
**ear** das Ohr [or]
  **I've got earache** ich habe Ohrenschmerzen [isн
hah-buh or-ren-shmairtsen]
**early** früh [frȫ]
  **we want to leave a day earlier** wir möchten
einen Tag früher abreisen [veer mursнten ine-en
tahg frȫ-er ap-ry-zen]
**earring** der Ohrring [or-ring]
**east** der Osten
**Easter** Ostern [o-stern]
**Easter Monday** Ostermontag [o-ster-mohntag]
**easy** leicht [lysнt]
**eat** essen
  **something to eat** etwas zu essen [etvass
tsoo...]
**EC, Eurocity** Euro Express
**egg** ein Ei [ɪ]
**Einbahnstraße** one-way street
**Einfahrt** entrance; motorway slip road
**Eingang** entrance
**Einordnen** get in lane
**Einstieg vorn/hinten** enter at the front/rear
**Eintritt frei** admission free
**either: either...or...** entweder...oder... [ent-vay-
der...o-der]

**I don't like either** mir gefällt beides nicht [meer geh-felt by-dess niSHt]

**elastic** elastisch

**elastic band** ein Gummiband [gɷmee-bant]

**elbow** der Ellbogen [el-bo-ghen]

**electric** elektrisch

**electric fire** ein elektrisches Heizgerät [...hites-gheh-rayt]

**electrician** der Elektriker

**electricity** die Elektrizität [elek-trits-i-tayt]

> ✈ Voltage in Germany is 220, as in the UK.
> But you will need to buy a plug adaptor
> before you leave. German plugs have two
> round pins.

**elegant** elegant [el-ay-gant]

**else: something else** etwas anderes [etvass...]

  **somewhere else** irgendwo anders [eer-ghent-vo...]

  **let's go somewhere else** gehen wir woanders hin! [gay-en veer vo-...]

  **who else?** wer sonst? [vair zonst]

  **or else** sonst

**email** eine E-Mail

  **why don't you email me?** schick mir doch eine E-Mail [...meer doKH ine-uh...]

**email address** die E-Mail-Adresse [-adressuh]

  **what's your email address?** was ist deine E-Mail-Adresse? [...dy-nuh...]

> *YOU MAY THEN HEAR*
> meine E-Mail-Adresse ist...
>   at...
>   Punkt ... [poonkt]
> *my email address is...*
>   *at...*
>   *dot...*

**embarrassed** verlegen [fair-lay-ghen]
**embarrassing** peinlich [pine-lisн]
**embassy** die Botschaft [boht-shafft]
**emergency** der Notfall [noht-fal]
**empty** leer [layr]
**end** das Ende [end-uh]
  **when does it end?** bis wann geht es? [biss van
  gayt ess]
**engaged** *(telephone, toilet)* besetzt [buh-zetst]
  *(person)* verlobt [fair-lohbt]
**engagement ring** der Verlobungsring [fair-
  lohbœngs-]
**engine** *(of car, plane)* der Motor [mo-tor]
**engine trouble** Schwierigkeiten mit dem Motor
  [shveerisн-kite-en mit daym mo-tor]
**England** England [eng-lant]
**English** englisch [eng-lish]
  **the English** die Engländer [eng-lender]
**Englishman** ein Engländer [eng-lender]
**Englishwoman** eine Engländerin
**enjoy: I enjoyed it very much** ich habe es sehr
  genossen [isн hah-buh ess zair gheh-nossen]
  **enjoy yourself** viel Spaß [feel shpass]
  **I enjoy riding/driving** ich reite/fahre gern [isн
  ry-tuh/faruh gairn]
**enlargement** *(photo)* eine Vergrößerung [fair-
  grurss-erœong]
**enormous** enorm [ay-norm]
**enough** genug [gheh-noog]
  **that's not big enough** das ist nicht groß
  genug [...nisнt grohss...]
  **I don't have enough money** ich habe nicht
  genug Geld [isн hah-buh...]
  **thank you, that's enough** danke, das ist genug
  [dankuh...]
**ensuite: is it ensuite?** ist das mit eigenem Bad?
  [...i-gheh-nem baht]

**entertainment** die Unterhaltung [ɔonter-halt-ɔong]

**entrance** der Eingang [ine-gang]
*(for vehicle)* die Einfahrt

**envelope** der Umschlag [ɔom-shlahg]

**Erdgeschoss** ground floor

**Erfrischungen** refreshments

**error** der Fehler [fayler]

**erste Hilfe** first aid

**Erwachsene** adults

**escalator** die Rolltreppe [-puh]

**especially** besonders [buh-zonders]

**essential** notwendig [noht-vendisн]

**e-ticket** ein E-Ticket [ay-]

**euro** ein Euro [oyro]

---

The Germans jokingly refer to the euro as the 'Teuro' (**teuer** means expensive).

---

**Europe** Europa [oyro-pa]

**even: even the British** sogar die Briten [zo-gar dee breeten]

**evening** der Abend [ah-bent]
  **in the evening** am Abend
  **this evening** heute Abend [hoytuh...]
  **good evening** guten Abend [gooten...]

**evening dress** *(for man)* der Abendanzug [ah-bent-an-tsoog]
  *(for woman)* das Abendkleid [-klite]

**ever: have you ever been to...?** sind Sie *jemals* in...gewesen? [zint zee yay-malss in...gheh-vay-zen]

**every** jeder [yay-der]
  **every day** jeden Tag [yay-den tahg]

**everyone** jeder [yay-der]
  **is everyone ready?** sind alle fertig? [zint al-uh fairtisн]

**everything** alles [al-ess]

**everywhere** überall [ōōber-al]
**exact** genau [gheh-now]
**example** das Beispiel [by-shpeel]
  **for example** zum Beispiel [tsōōm...]
**excellent** ausgezeichnet [owss-gheh-tsysH-net]
**except: except me** außer mir [owss-er meer]
**excess baggage** Übergewicht [ōōber-gheh-visHt]
**exchange rate** der Wechselkurs [veksel-kōōrss]
**excursion** der Ausflug [owss-floog]
**excuse me** Entschuldigung! [ent-shōōl-digōōng]
**exhaust** *(on car)* der Auspuff [owss-poof]
**exhausted** erschöpft [air-shurpft]
**exhibition** die Ausstellung [owss-shtel-ōōng]
**exit** der Ausgang [owss-gang]
  *(for vehicle)* die Ausfahrt
**expect: she's expecting** sie ist in anderen
  Umständen [zee ist in an-duh-ren ōōm-shtenden]
**expenses: it's on expenses** das geht auf Spesen
  [dass gayt owf shpay-zen]
**expensive** teuer [toy-er]
**expert** der Experte [ekspair-tuh]
  *(woman)* die Expertin
**explain** erklären [air-klairen]
  **would you explain that very slowly?** können
  Sie das ganz langsam erklären? [kurnen zee dass
  gants lang-zahm...]
**extra: an extra day** ein Tag extra [ine tahg...]
  **is that extra?** wird das extra berechnet? [veert
  dass...buh-resH-net]
**extremely** äußerst [oysserst]
**eye** das Auge [ow-guh]
**eyebrow** die Augenbraue [ow-ghen-brow-uh]
**eyebrow pencil** ein Augenbrauenstift [ow-ghen-brow-en-shtift]
**eyeliner** ein 'Eyeliner'
**eye shadow** der Lidschatten [leet-shat-en]

**eye witness** der Augenzeuge [ow-ghen-tsoy-guh]
  *(woman)* die Augenzeugin

# F [eff]

**face** das Gesicht [gheh-ziSHt]
**fact** die Tatsache [taht-zahKH-uh]
**factory** die Fabrik [fab-reek]
**Fahrenheit** Fahrenheit

> ✈ F - 32 x 5/9 = C

| Fahrenheit | 23 | 32 | 50 | 59 | 70 | 86 | 98.4 |
|---|---|---|---|---|---|---|---|
| centigrade | -5 | 0 | 10 | 15 | 21 | 30 | 36.9 |

**Fahrkarten** tickets
**Fahrscheine** tickets
**faint: she's fainted** sie ist ohnmächtig geworden
  [zee ist ohn-meSH-tiSH gheh-vorden]
**fair** *(fun-)* der Jahrmarkt [yahr-]
  *(commercial)* die Messe [mess-uh]
  **that's not fair** das ist nicht fair
**fake** eine Fälschung [felshœng]
**fall: he's fallen** er ist gefallen [air ist gheh-fal-en]
**false** falsch
**false teeth** ein Gebiss [gheh-biss]
**family** die Familie [fam-ee-lee-uh]
**fan** *(cooling)* der Ventilator [-ah-tor]
  *(supporter)* der Fan [fen]
**fan belt** der Keilriemen [kile-reemen]
**far** weit [vite]
  **is it far?** ist es weit?
  **how far is it?** wie weit ist es? [vee…]
**fare** *(travel)* der Fahrpreis [far-price]
  *(by air)* der Flugpreis [floog-price]
**farm** der Bauernhof [bow-ern-hohff]
**farther** weiter [vyter]
**fashion** die Mode [mo-duh]
**fast** *(adjective)* schnell [shnel]

**don't speak so fast** sprechen Sie nicht so
schnell! [shpresHen zee nisHt zo...]
**fat** *(adjective)* dick
**father: my father** mein Vater [mine fahter]
**fault** *(defect)* der Fehler [fayler]
 **it's not my fault** das ist nicht meine Schuld
 [dass ist nisHt mine-uh shoolt]
**faulty** defekt [dayfekt]
**favourite** *(adjective)* Lieblings- [leeplings]
**fax** das Fax
 **can you fax this for me?** können Sie das für
 mich faxen? [kurnen zee dass foor misH faksen]
**February** Februar [fay-broo-ar]
**fed-up: I'm fed-up** ich habe die Nase voll [isH
 hah-buh dee nah-zuh fol]
**feel: I feel like a...** *(I want)* ich habe Lust auf
 ein... [isH hah-buh loost owf ine]
Feierabend we're closing
**felt-tip** ein Filzstift [filts-shtift]
Fernsprecher telephone
**ferry** die Fähre [fay-ruh]
**fetch: will you come and fetch me?** werden Sie
 mich abholen? [vairden zee mich ap-ho-len]
**fever** das Fieber [feeber]
**few: only a few** nur ein paar [noor ine par]
 **a few days** ein paar Tage [...tah-guh]
**fiancé** der Verlobte [fair-lohp-ter]
**fiancée** die Verlobte [fair-lohp-tuh]
**fiddle: it's a fiddle** das ist Schiebung [dass ist
 shee-boong]
**field** das Feld [felt]
 *(grass)* die Wiese [vee-zuh]
**fifty-fifty** 'fifty-fifty'
**figure** *(number)* die Zahl [tsahl]
 *(of person)* die Figur [figoor]
**fill: fill her up** voll tanken, bitte [fol tanken bittuh]
 **to fill in a form** ein Formular ausfüllen [...owss-

fool-en]

**fillet** das Filet [feelay]

**filling** *(in tooth)* die Plombe [plom-buh]

**film** der Film

 **do you have this type of film?** haben Sie solche Filme? [hah-ben zee zolsнuh…]

**filter** der Filter

**find** finden [fin-den]

 **if you find it** wenn Sie es finden [ven zee ess…]

 **I've found a…** ich habe ein…gefunden [isн hah-buh ine…gheh-foonden]

**fine** *(weather)* schön [shurn]

 **ok, that's fine** das ist gut [dass ist goot]

 **a fifty euro fine** eine Geldbuße von fünfzig Euro [ine-uh ghelt-boo-zuh fon foonf-tsisн oyro]

**finger** der Finger [fing-er]

**fingernail** der Fingernagel [fing-er-nah-ghel]

**finish: I haven't finished** ich bin noch nicht fertig [isн bin noкн nisнt fairtisн]

 **when does it finish?** bis wann geht es? [biss van gayt ess]

**fire** ein Feuer [foy-er]

 *(house on fire etc)* ein Brand [brant]

 **fire!** Feuer! [foy-er]

 **can we light a fire here?** können wir hier ein Feuer machen? [kurnen veer heer ine foy-er mahкнen]

 **it's not firing** *(car)* es zündet nicht [ess tsoondet nisнt]

**fire brigade** die Feuerwehr [foy-er-vair]

✈ Dial 112.

**fire extinguisher** der Feuerlöscher [foy-er-lursher]

**first** erste [air-stuh]

 **I was first** *(in queue)* ich war zuerst hier [isн var

tsoo-airst heer]
**first aid** erste Hilfe [air-stuh hilf-uh]
**first aid kit** der Verbandskasten [fair-bants-]
**first class** *(travel)* erste Klasse [...klass-uh]
**first name** der Vorname [for-nah-muh]
**fish** der Fisch [fish]
**fishing** das Angeln [ang-eln]
**fishing rod** eine Angelrute [ang-el-rootuh]
**fit** *(healthy)* gesund [gheh-zoont]
  *(in shape)* gut in Form [goot...]
  **it doesn't fit me** es passt mir nicht [...meer nisHt]
**fix: can you fix it?** *(repair)* können Sie das in Ordnung bringen? [kurnen zee dass in ordnoong...]
**fizzy** mit Kohlensäure [mit kohlen-zoy-ruh]
**flag** die Fahne [fah-nuh]
  *(national, ship's)* die Flagge [flag-uh]
**flash** *(photography)* das Blitzlicht [-lisHt]
**flat** *(adjective)* flach [flahKH]
  *(apartment)* die Wohnung [vo-noong]
  **I've got a flat (tyre)** ich habe einen Platten [isH hah-buh ine-en...]
**flavour** der Geschmack [gheh-shmack]
**flea** der Floh
**flies** *(on trousers)* der Reißverschluss [rice-fair-shlooss]
**flight** der Flug [floog]
**flight number** die Flugnummer [floog-noomer]
**flirt** *(verb)* flirten [flurten]
**float** *(verb)* schwimmen [shvimmen]
**floor** der Boden [bo-den]
  **on the second floor** im zweiten Stock [...tsvy-ten shtock]
**flower** eine Blume [bloom-uh]
**flu** die Grippe [grip-uh]
**Flug** flight

**Flugsteig** gate
**fly** *(insect)* die Fliege [fleeg-uh]
  *(verb)* fliegen [fleeghen]
**foggy** neblig [nay-blisH]
**follow** folgen [fol-ghen]
**food** das Essen
  *(groceries)* die Lebensmittel [lay-benz-]
  **we'd like to eat German-style food** wir
  würden gerne etwas typisch Deutsches essen
  [veer vöörden gairn-uh etvass töopish doytshess…]
**food poisoning** eine Lebensmittelvergiftung [lay-
  benz-mittel-fair-ghif-töong]
**fool** der Narr
  *(female)* die Närrin [nerrin]
**foot** der Fuß [fooss]

✈ 1 foot = 30.5 cm = 0.3 metres

**football** der Fußball [fooss-bal]
**for** für [föor]
  **that's for me** das ist für mich
**forbidden** verboten [fair-bo-ten]
**foreign** ausländisch [owss-lend-ish]
**foreign currency** Devisen [day-veezen]
**foreigner** ein Ausländer [owss-lender]
  *(woman)* eine Ausländerin
**forest** der Wald [valt]
**forget** vergessen [fair-ghessen]
  **I forget** ich weiß nicht mehr [isH vice nisHt mair]
  **I've forgotten** ich habe es vergessen [isH hah-
  buh ess…]
  **don't forget** vergessen Sie es nicht […zee ess
  nisHt]
**fork** *(to eat with)* eine Gabel [gah-bel]
**form** *(document)* ein Formular [form-oo-lar]
**formal** formell
  *(person)* förmlich [furm-lisH]
**fortnight** vierzehn Tage [feer-tsayn tah-guh]

**forward** *(move etc)* vorwärts [for-vairts]
  **could you forward my mail?** könnten Sie mir
  die Post nachsenden? [kurnten zee meer dee
  posst nahKH-zenden]
**forwarding address** die Nachsendeadresse
  [nahKH-zenduh-ad-ressuh]
**foundation cream** eine Grundierungscreme
  [groon-deer-roongs-kraym]
**fountain** der Brunnen [broonen]
**four-wheel drive** ein Wagen mit Allradantrieb
  [vah-ghen mit al-raht-an-treep]
**fracture** der Bruch [brooKH]
**fragile** zerbrechlich [tsair-bresH-lisH]
**France** Frankreich [frank-rysH]
**fraud** der Betrug [buh-troog]
**free** frei [fry]
  **admission free** Eintritt frei [ine-]
**frei** vacant; free
**Freibad** open-air pool
**freight** die Fracht [frahKHt]
**Fremdenverkehrsamt** tourist information office
**Fremdenzimmer** rooms to rent
**French** französisch [frants-ur-zish]
**fresh** frisch
**freshen up: I'd like to freshen up** ich möchte
  mich frisch machen [isH mursHtuh misH frish
  mahKHen]
**Friday** Freitag [fry-tahg]
**fridge** der Kühlschrank [kool-shrank]
**fried egg** ein Spiegelei [shpee-ghel-I]
**friend** ein Freund [froynt]
  *(female)* eine Freundin [froyndin]
**friendly** freundlich [froynt-lisH]
**fries** die Pommes frites [pom frit]
**from** von [fon]
  **from England/London** aus England/London
  [owss eng-lant...]

**where is it from?** wo kommt es her? [vo...ess hair]

**front: in front of you** vor Ihnen [for ee-nen]

**at the front** vorn [forn]

**frost** der Frost

**frostbite** die Frostbeule [-boy-luh]

**fruit** das Obst [ohpst]

**fruit salad** ein Obstsalat [ohpst-zal-aht]

**fry** braten [brah-ten]

**nothing fried** nichts Gebratenes [nisнts gheh-brah-ten-ess]

**frying pan** die Bratpfanne [braht-pfan-uh]

**full** voll [fol]

**fun: it's fun** das macht Spaß [dass mahкнt shpahss]

**have fun!** viel Spaß! [feel...]

**Fundbüro** lost property

**funny** (strange, comical) komisch [ko-mish]

**furniture** die Möbel [mur-bel]

**further** weiter [vyter]

**fuse** die Sicherung [zisнer-œng]

**future** die Zukunft [tsoo-kœnft]

**in future** in Zukunft

# G [gay]

**gale** der Sturm [shtoorm]

**gallon** die Gallone [gal-o-nuh]

✈ 1 gallon = 4.55 litres

**gallstone** ein Gallenstein [gal-en-shtine]

**gamble** spielen [shpeelen]

(on horses etc) wetten [vet-en]

**garage** (for repairs) die Werkstatt [vairk-shtat]

(for petrol) die Tankstelle [-shtel-uh]

(for parking) die Garage [ga-rah-juh]

✈ Garages can be good places to buy supplies since there aren't any 24-hour shops.

**garden** der Garten
**garlic** der Knoblauch [kuh-nohp-lowKH]
**gas** das Gas [gahss]
  *(petrol)* das Benzin [ben-tseen]
**gas cylinder** der Gaszylinder [gahss-tsoo-linder]
**gasket** die Dichtung [diSH-toong]
**gay** schwul [shvool]
**gear** *(in car)* der Gang
  *(equipment)* die Ausrüstung [owss-rōōs-toong]
  **I can't get it into gear** ich kann den Gang nicht einlegen [iSH kan dayn...nisHt ine-lay-ghen]
**Gebühren** charges
**Gefahr** danger
**Gegenverkehr** oncoming traffic
**gents** die Herrentoilette [hair-ren-twalet-uh]
**geöffnet** open
**Gepäckaufbewahrung** left luggage
**German** deutsch [doytsh]
  **a German** *(man)* ein Deutscher [doytsh-er]
  *(woman)* eine Deutsche [doytsh-uh]
  **the Germans** die Deutschen
  **I don't speak German** ich spreche kein Deutsch [iSH shpresH-uh kine...]
**Germany** Deutschland [doytsh-lant]
**geschlossen** closed
**Geschwindigkeitsbegrenzung** speed limit
**gesture** eine Geste [gay-stuh]
**get: will you get me a...?** holen Sie mir bitte ein...? [ho-len zee meer bittuh ine]
  **how do I get to...?** wie komme ich zu...? [vee kom-uh iSH tsoo]
  **where do I get a bus for...?** wo fährt der Bus nach...ab? [vo fairt dair booss nahKH...ap]

**when can I get it back?** wann bekomme ich es zurück? [van buh-kom-uh isH ess tsoo-röock]

**when do we get back?** wann sind wir zurück? [van zint veer tsoo-röock]

**where do I get off?** wo muss ich aussteigen? [vo mooss isH owss-shty-ghen]

**have you got...?** haben Sie...? [hah-ben zee] *(familiar)* hast du...? [...doo]

**gin** ein 'Gin'

**gin and tonic** ein 'Gin Tonic'

**girl** ein Mädchen [mayd-sHen]

**girlfriend** die Freundin [froyndin]

**give** geben [gay-ben]

**will you give me...?** geben Sie mir bitte... [...zee meer bittuh]

**I gave it to him** ich habe es ihm gegeben [isH hah-buh ess eem gheh-gay-ben]

**glad** froh

**glass** das Glas

**a glass of water** ein Glas Wasser [...vasser]

**glasses** die Brille [bril-uh]

**Glatteis** black ice

**Gleis** platform

**glue** der Klebstoff [klayp-shtoff]

**Glühwein** mulled wine

**GmbH, Gesellschaft mit beschränkter Haftung** Ltd.

**go** gehen [gay-en]

*(by vehicle)* fahren

**I want to go to Heidelberg** ich möchte nach Heidelberg [isH mursHtuh nahkH...]

**when does the bus go?** wann fährt der Bus? [van fairt dair booss]

**he's gone** er ist weg [air ist vek]

**where are you going?** wo gehen Sie hin? [vo...zee...]

**let's go** gehen wir! [...veer]

**go on!** los! [lohss]
**can I have a go?** kann ich es versuchen? [kan
iSH ess fair-zooKHen]
**goal** das Tor
**God** Gott
**goggles** *(for skiing)* die Schneebrille [shnay-bril-
uh]
**gold** das Gold [golt]
**golf** Golf
**good** gut [goot]
  **good!** gut!
**goodbye** auf Wiedersehen [owf veeder-zayn]
**got: have you got...?** haben Sie...? [hah-ben zee]
  *(familiar)* hast du...? [...doo]
**gram** ein Gramm
**granddaughter** die Enkelin [eng-kel-in]
**grandfather** der Großvater [grohssfahter]
**grandmother** die Großmutter [grohss-
mooter]
**grandson** der Enkel
**grapefruit** eine 'Grapefruit'
**grapefruit juice** ein Grapefruitsaft [-zaft]
**grapes** Trauben [trow-ben]
**grass** das Gras [grahss]
**grateful: I'm very grateful to you** ich bin Ihnen
sehr *dankbar* [iSH bin ee-nen zair...]
**gravy** die Soße [zo-suh]
**grease** das Fett
  *(for machinery)* die Wagenschmiere [vah-ghen-
shmeeruh]
**greasy** fettig
**great** groß [grohss]
  *(very good)* großartig [grohss-artiSH]
  **great!** klasse! [klas-suh]
**Greece** Griechenland [greeSHen-lant]
**greedy** gierig [ghee-riSH]
  *(for food)* gefräßig [geh-fraysiSH]

**green** grün [grōōn]
**grey** grau [grow]
**grocer's** der Kaufmann [kowf-]
**ground** der Boden [bo-den]
  **on the ground** auf dem Boden [owf daym…]
  **on the ground floor** im Erdgeschoss […airt-gheh-shoss]
**group** die Gruppe [grōōp-uh]
  **our group leader** unser Gruppenleiter [ōōn-zer grōōpen-ly-ter]
  *(woman)* unsere Gruppenleiterin
  **I'm with the English group** ich gehöre zur englischen Gruppe [iSH gheh-hur-uh tsoor english-en…]
**guarantee** eine Garantie
  **is there a guarantee?** ist darauf Garantie? […darowf…]
**guest** ein Gast
**guesthouse** eine Pension [pen-zee-ohn]
**guide** der Führer [fōōrer]
  *(woman)* die Führerin
**guidebook** ein Reiseführer [ry-zuh-fōōrer]
**guided tour** eine Rundfahrt [rōōnt-fart]
  *(on foot)* ein Rundgang
**guilty** schuldig [shōōl-diSH]
**guitar** die Gitarre [ghee-taruh]
**gum** *(in mouth)* der Gaumen [gow-men]
**gun** *(pistol)* die Pistole [-o-luh]

# H [hah]

**hair** das Haar [har]
**hairbrush** die Haarbürste [har-bōōr-stuh]
**haircut: where can I get a haircut?** wo kann ich mir die Haare schneiden lassen? [vo kan iSH meer dee hah-ruh shnyden lassen]
**hairdresser's: is there a hairdresser's here?** gibt

es hier einen Friseur? [gheept ess heer ine-en free-zur]

✈ Normally shut on Mondays.

**hair grip** die Haarklemme [har-klem-uh]
**half** halb [halp]
   **a half portion** halbe Portion [halbuh portsee-ohn]
   **half an hour** eine halbe Stunde [...shtoon-duh]
   *go to* time
**ham** der Schinken
**hamburger** ein Hamburger
**hammer** ein Hammer
**hand** die Hand [hant]
**handbag** eine Handtasche [hant-tash-uh]
**hand baggage** das Handgepäck [hant-gheh-peck]
**handbrake** die Handbremse [hant-brem-zuh]
**handkerchief** das Taschentuch [tash-en-tooкн]
**handle** der Griff
   *(of cup)* der Henkel
**handmade** handgearbeitet [hant-gheh-ar-by-tet]
**handsome** gutaussehend [goot-owss-zay-ent]
**hanger** der Kleiderbügel [kly-der-bōō-gel]
**hangover** der Kater [kahter]
**happen** passieren [pas-eeren]
   **I don't know how it happened** ich weiß nicht, wie es passiert ist [isн vice nisнt vee ess pas-eert...]
   **what's happening?** was ist los? [vass ist lohss]
   **what's happened?** was ist passiert?
**happy** glücklich [glōōck-lisн]
**harbour** der Hafen [hah-fen]
**hard** hart
   *(difficult)* schwierig [shveerisн]
**hard-boiled egg** ein hartgekochtes Ei [hart-gheh-koкн-tess I]
**harm** der Schaden [shah-den]

**hat** der Hut [hoot]
**hate: I hate...** ich hasse... [isн hass-uh]
**have** haben [hah-ben]
    **can I have some water?** kann ich etwas Wasser
    haben? [kan isн etvass vasser...]
    **I have no...** ich habe kein... [isн hah-buh kine]
    **do you have any cigars/a map?** haben Sie
    Zigarren/eine Karte? [hah-ben zee...]
    **I have to leave tomorrow** ich muss morgen
    abreisen [isн mooss mor-ghen ap-ry-zen]

> Here is the present tense of the German
> verb for 'to have'.
>
> **I have** ich habe [isн hah-buh]
> **you have** (familiar) du hast [doo...]
> **you have** (polite) Sie haben [zee hah-ben]
> **he/she/it has** er/sie/es hat [air/zee/ess...]
> **we have** wir haben [veer...]
> **you have** (familiar plural) ihr habt [eer...]
> **you have** (polite plural) Sie haben
> **they have** sie haben

**hay fever** der Heuschnupfen [hoy-shnoop-fen]
**Hbf, Hauptbahnhof** central station
**he** er [air]
**head** der Kopf
**headache** Kopfschmerzen [kopf-shmairtsen]
**headlight** der Scheinwerfer [shine-vairfer]

> ✈ Flashing headlights will mostly mean 'stop'
> or 'get out of my way' and NOT 'after you,
> chum' as in the UK.

**head waiter** der Oberkellner [ohber-]
**health** die Gesundheit [gheh-zoont-hite]
    **your health!** auf Ihr Wohl! [owf eer vohl]
**hear: I can't hear** ich höre nichts [isн hur-uh
nisнts]

**hearing aid** das Hörgerät [hur-gheh-rayt]
**heart** das Herz [hairts]
**heart attack** ein Herzinfarkt [hairts-]
**heat** die Hitze [hit-suh]
**heating** die Heizung [hitesoong]
**heat stroke** ein Hitzschlag [hits-shlahg]
**heavy** schwer [shvair]
**heel** die Ferse [fairsuh]
  *(of shoe)* der Absatz [ap-zats]
  **could you put new heels on these?** könnten
  Sie neue Absätze darauf machen? [kurnten zee
  noy-uh ap-zets-uh darowf maнкнen]
**height** die Höhe [hur-uh]
  *(person's)* die Größe [grur-suh]
**heiß** hot
**hello** hallo
  *(on phone)* hallo

> You will also hear **guten Tag** or just **Tag**.
> And in the south of Germany: **grüß Gott**.

**help** die Hilfe [hilf-uh]
  **can you help me?** würden Sie mir helfen?
  [vo͞orden zee meer...]
  **help!** Hilfe!
**her**[1] : **I know her** ich kenne *sie* [...zee]
  **will you give it to her?** würden Sie es *ihr*
  geben? [vo͞orden zee ess eer gay-ben]
  **with her** mit ihr
  **for her** für sie
  **it's her** sie ist es
  **who? – her** wer? – sie
**her**[2] *(possessive)* ihr/ihre/ihr [eer/eer-uh...]

> These forms correspond to the articles
> **der/die/das**. The plural is **ihre**.
>   **it's her bag** es ist ihre Tasche [ess ist eer-
>   uh tash-uh]

**here** hier [heer]
  **come here** komm her! [...hair]
**Herren** gents
**hers** ihrer/ihre/ihres [eer-er/eer-uh/eer-ess]

> These forms correspond to the articles
> **der/die/das**. The plural is **ihre**.

**hi!** hallo!
**high** hoch [hohKH]
  **higher up** höher [hur-er]
**high chair** ein Hochstuhl [hohKH-shtool]
**hill** der Berg [bairk]
  *(on road)* die Steigung [shty-goong]
  **up/down the hill** den Berg hinauf/hinunter
  [dayn...hin-owf/hin-oonter]
**him: I know him** ich kenne *ihn* [...een]
  **will you give it to him?** würden Sie es *ihm*
  geben? [vöörden zee ess eem gay-ben]
  **with him** mit ihm
  **for him** für ihn
  **it's him** er ist es [air ist ess]
  **who? – him** wer? – er
**hire** *go to* **rent**
**his** sein/seine/sein [zine/zine-uh...]

> These forms correspond to the articles
> **der/die/das**. The plural is **seine**.
>   **it's his drink** es ist sein Drink
>   **it's his** es ist seiner/seine/seins [zine-er/
>   zine-uh/zine-ss]

**hit: he hit me** er hat mich geschlagen [air hat
  misH gheh-shlah-ghen]
**hitch-hike** trampen [trempen]
**hitch-hiker** der Anhalter
  *(female)* die Anhalterin
**Hochgarage** multi-storey car park
**Höchstgeschwindigkeit** maximum speed

**hold** *(verb)* halten
**hole** das Loch [loкн]
**holiday** der Urlaub [oor-lowp]
  *(single day)* ein Feiertag [fy-er-tahg]
  **I'm on holiday** ich bin im Urlaub
**Holland** Holland [hol-ant]
**home** das Zuhause [tsoo-how-zuh]
  **at home** zu Hause
  **I want to go home** ich möchte nach Hause [isн
  mursнtuh nahкн how-zuh]
**homesick: I'm homesick** ich habe Heimweh [isн
  hah-buh hime-vay]
**honest** ehrlich [air-lisн]
**honestly?** ehrlich? [air-lisн]
**honey** der Honig [ho-nisн]
**honeymoon** die Hochzeitsreise [hoнкн-tsites-ry-
  zuh]
**hope** die Hoffnung [hoff-nɔong]
  **I hope that...** ich hoffe, dass... [isн hoff-uh dass]
  **I hope so** hoffentlich! [hoff-ent-lisн]
  **I hope not** hoffentlich nicht! [...nisнт]
**horn** *(of car)* die Hupe [hoop-uh]
**horrible** schrecklich [shreck-lisн]
**horse** das Pferd [pfairt]
**hospital** das Krankenhaus [kranken-howss]

> ✈ Reciprocal health agreement gives free
> hospital treatment in Germany but not for
> the first 14 days of hospital treatment. Get
> a form E111 from your local post office
> before you leave.

**host** der Gastgeber [-gay-ber]
**hostess** die Gastgeberin [-gay-berin]
**hot** heiß [hice]
  *(spiced)* scharf [sharf]
  **I'm so hot!** mir ist so heiß! [meer...]
  **it's so hot today!** es ist so heiß heute! [...zo...

hoytuh]
**hotel** das Hotel
  **at my hotel** in meinem Hotel

> ✈ As well as hotels, cheaper options are a
> **Pension** (boarding house) or a **Gasthof**
> (inn). If you want a room in a private
> house, look for the sign **Zimmer frei** or
> **Fremdenzimmer**. You can get information
> on local accommodation from the tourist
> information office.

**hour** eine Stunde [shtoonduh]
**house** das Haus [howss]
**how** wie [vee]
  **how many?** wie viele? [vee-feel-uh]
  **how much?** wie viel? [vee-feel]
  **how much is it?** was kostet das? [vass…]
  **how long?** wie lange? [vee lang-uh]
  **how long have you been here?** seit wann sind
  Sie da? [zite van zint zee da]
  **how are you?** wie geht's? […gayts]

> *YOU MAY THEN HEAR*
> gut danke *fine thanks*
> geht so *so-so*

**humid** feucht [foysHt]
**hungry: I'm hungry** ich habe Hunger [isH hah-
buh hoong-er]
  **I'm not hungry** ich habe keinen Hunger
  […kine-en…]
**hupen** sound your horn
**hurry: I'm in a hurry** ich habe es eilig [isH hah-
buh ess I-lisH]
  **please hurry!** bitte beeilen Sie sich! [bittuh buh-
I-len zee zisH]
**hurt: it hurts** es tut weh [ess toot vay]
  **my leg hurts** mein Bein tut mir weh [mine bine

toot meer vay]
**husband: my husband** mein Mann

# I [ee]

**I** ich [iSH]
**IC** Intercity
**ice** das Eis [ice]
  **with lots of ice** mit viel Eis [mit feel...]
**ice-axe** der Eispickel [ice-]
**ice cream** das Eis [ice]
**identity papers** die Ausweispapiere [owss-vice-papee-ruh]
**idiot** ein Idiot [id-ee-oht]
  *(female)* eine Idiotin
**if** wenn [ven]
**ignition** *(of car)* die Zündung [tsŏŏn-dŏong]
**ill** krank
  **I feel ill** ich fühle mich nicht wohl [iSH fōō-luh miSH niSHt vohl]
**illegal** illegal [ilay-gahl]
**illegible** unleserlich [ŏŏn-lay-zair-liSH]
**illness** eine Krankheit [krank-hite]
**Imbissstube** snackbar
**immediately** sofort [zo-fort]
**important** wichtig [viSH-tiSH]
  **it's very important** es ist sehr wichtig [ess ist zair...]
**impossible** unmöglich [ŏŏn-mur-gliSH]
**impressive** beeindruckend [buh-ine-drŏock-ent]
**improve** verbessern [fairbessern]
  **I want to improve my German** ich möchte besser Deutsch lernen [iSH murSHtuh besser doytsh lair-nen]
**in** in
  **is he in?** ist er da? [...air...]

> The German word **in** together with **der** or
> **das** often becomes **im**.
>   **in the summer** im Sommer

**inch** der Zoll [tsol]

✈ 1 inch = 2.54 cm

**include** einschließen [ine-shleess-en]
  **does that include breakfast?** ist das Frühstück
  *inbegriffen?* [...frōō-shtōōck in-buh-]
**incompetent** unfähig [ōōn-fay-isн]
**inconsiderate** unaufmerksam [ōōn-owf-mairk-
  zahm]
**incredible** unglaublich [ōōn-glowp-lisн]
**indecent** unanständig [ōōn-an-shtendisн]
**independent** unabhängig [ōōn-ap-heng-isн]
**India** Indien [in-dee-un]
**indicate: he turned without indicating** er bog
  ab, ohne zu blinken [air bohg ap o-nuh tsoo...]
  *(cyclist)* er bog ab, ohne Zeichen zu geben
  [...tsy-sнen tsoo gay-ben]
**indicator** *(on car)* der Blinker
**indigestion** die Magenverstimmung [mah-ghen-
  fair-shtimōōng]
**indoors** drinnen
**infection** die Infektion [in-fekts-ee-ohn]
**infectious** ansteckend [an-shteck-ent]
**information** Informationen [informats-ee-o-nen]
  **do you have any information in English
  about...?** haben Sie Informationsmaterial in
  Englisch über...? [...mah-tay-ree-ahl in eng-lish
  ōōber]
  **is there an information office?** gibt es da
  eine Informationsstelle? [gheept ess da ine-uh
  informats-ee-ohns-shtel-uh]
**injection** die Spritze [shprits-uh]
**injured** verletzt [fair-letst]

**injury** die Verletzung [fair-lets∞ng]
**Inland** domestic; internal
**innocent** unschuldig [∞n-sh∞l-disH]
**insect** ein Insekt [inzekt]
**inside** innen
**insist: I insist** ich bestehe darauf [isH buh-shtay-uh darowf]
**insomnia** die Schlaflosigkeit [shlahf-lohs-isH-kite]
**instant coffee** der Pulverkaffee [p∞l-ver-kafay]
**instead** stattdessen [shtat-dessen]
  **instead of...** anstelle von... [an-shtel-uh fon]
**insulating tape** das Isolierband [eezoleer-bant]
**insult** die Beleidigung [buh-lide-ig∞ng]
**insurance** die Versicherung [fair-zisH-er∞ng]
**insurance company** die Versicherung [fair-zisH-er∞ng]
**intelligent** intelligent [-ghent]
**interesting** interessant [-ant]
**international** international [internats-ee-o-nahl]
**Internet** das Internet
**Internet café** ein Internetcafé [-kafay]
**interpret** dolmetschen [dolmet-shen]
  **would you interpret for us?** würden Sie für uns dolmetschen? [v∞rden zee f∞r ∞nss...]
**interpreter** ein Dolmetscher [dolmet-sher] *(woman)* eine Dolmetscherin
**into** in
  **I'm not into that** *(don't like)* ich steh' nicht darauf [isH shtay nisHt darowf]
**introduce: can I introduce...?** darf ich... vorstellen? [...for-shtellen]
**invalid** *(disabled)* der Invalide [in-val-eeduh] *(female)* die Invalidin
**invitation** eine Einladung [ine-lah-d∞ng]
  **thanks for the invitation** danke für die Einladung [dankuh f∞r dee...]
**invite: can I invite you out tonight?** kann ich

Sie für heute Abend einladen? [kan isH zee foor hoytuh ah-bent ine-lah-den]

**Ireland** Irland [eer-lant]

**Irish** irisch [eer-ish]

**iron** *(for clothes)* das Bügeleisen [boo-ghel-ı-zen]

**will you iron these for me?** würden Sie diese für mich bügeln? [voorden zee deez-uh foor misH boo-gheln]

**is** *go to* **be**

**island** die Insel [in-zel]

**it** es [ess]

**it is...** es ist...

**Italy** Italien [i-tahl-ee-un]

**itch: it itches** es juckt [ess yoockt]

**itemize: would you itemize it for me?** würden Sie dies für mich *aufschlüsseln*? [voorden zee deess foor misH owf-shlooss-eln]

# J [yot]

**jack** *(for car)* der Wagenheber [vah-ghen-hayber]

**jacket** die Jacke [yack-uh]

**jam** die Marmelade [marmuh-lah-duh]

**traffic jam** der (Verkehrs)stau [fair-kairs-shtow]

**January** Januar [yan-oo-ar]

**jaw** der Kiefer [keefer]

**jealous** eifersüchtig [ı-fair-zoosH-tisH]

**jeans** die Jeans

**jellyfish** die Qualle [kval-uh]

**jetty** der Pier

**jewellery** der Schmuck [shmoock]

**job** die Arbeit [ar-bite]

**just the job** goldrichtig [golt-risH-tisH]

**joke** der Witz [vits]

**you must be joking!** das soll wohl ein Witz sein! [dass zol vohl ine vits zine]

**journey** die Reise [ry-zuh]

**have a good journey!** gute Reise! [goot-uh...]
**Jugendherberge** youth hostel
**July** Juli [yoo-lee]
**junction** die Kreuzung [kroy-tsoong]
  *(M-way)* das Autobahnkreuz [owto-bahn-kroyts]
**June** Juni [yoo-nee]
**junk** der Ramsch [ramsh]
  *(food)* der Mist
**just** *(only)* nur [noor]
  *(exactly)* genau [gheh-now]
  **just two** nur zwei
  **just there** genau dort
  **just a little** nur ein wenig [...vayniSH]
  **not just now** jetzt nicht [yets nisHt]
  **just now** jetzt
  **he was here just now** er war gerade hier [air var gheh-rah-duh heer]
  **that's just right** das ist gerade richtig [dass ist gheh-rah-duh riSH-tiSH]

# K [kah]

**kalt** cold
**Kasse** cash desk
**kebab** der Schaschlik [shash-lik]
  **donner kebab** der Dönerkebab [durner-]
**keep: can I keep it?** kann ich es behalten? [...buh-halten]
  **you keep it** Sie können es behalten [zee kurnen...]
  **keep the change** stimmt so [shtimt zo]
  **you didn't keep your promise** Sie haben Ihr Versprechen nicht gehalten [zee hah-ben eer fair-shpreSHen nisHt gheh-halten]
  **it keeps on breaking** es geht dauernd kaputt [ess gayt dow-ernt...]
**kein Durchgang für Fußgänger** no pedestrians

**kein Einstieg** no entrance
**kein Trinkwasser** not for drinking
**kein Zutritt (für Unbefugte)** no admittance (for unauthorized persons)
**Keller** basement; cellar
**key** der Schlüssel [shlⲟⲟssel]
**keycard** eine Schlüsselkarte [shlⲟⲟssel-kartuh]
**kidney** die Niere [neer-uh]
**kill** töten [tur-ten]
**kilo** ein Kilo

✈ kilos/5 x 11 = pounds

| kilos | 1 | 1.5 | 5 | 6 | 7 | 8 | 9 |
|---|---|---|---|---|---|---|---|
| pounds | 2.2 | 3.3 | 11 | 13.2 | 15.4 | 17.6 | 19.8 |

**kilometre** ein Kilometer [keelo-mayter]

✈ kilometres/8 x 5 = miles

| kilometres | 1 | 5 | 10 | 20 | 50 | 100 |
|---|---|---|---|---|---|---|
| miles | | 0.62 | 3.1 | 6.2 | 12.4 | 31 | 62 |

**kind: that's very kind of you** das ist sehr *freundlich* von Ihnen [...zair froynt-lisн fon ee-nen]
  **what kind of...?** was für ein..? [vass fⲟⲟr ine]
**kiss** der Kuss [kⲟⲟss]
  *(verb)* küssen [kⲟⲟssen]
**kitchen** die Küche [kⲟⲟsн-uh]
**knee** das Knie [kuh-nee]
**knife** ein Messer
**knock** *(verb: at door)* klopfen
  **there's a knocking noise from the engine** der Motor klopft
**know** wissen [vissen]
  *(person, place)* kennen
  **I don't know** ich weiß nicht [isн vice nisнt]
  **I didn't know** ich wusste nicht [...vⲟⲟstuh...]
  **I don't know the area** ich kenne die Gegend nicht

**Krankenhaus** hospital
**Kreuzung** crossroads
**kurvenreiche Strecke** bends

# L [el]

**label** das Etikett
**laces** Schnürsenkel [shnœr-zenkel]
**lacquer** der Lack
**ladies (toilet)** die Damentoilette [dah-men-twalet-uh]
**lady** eine Dame [dah-muh]
**lager** ein helles Bier [...beer]
  **a lager and lime** ein helles Bier mit Limonensirup

✈ Not a German drink. You could ask for 'eine Berliner Weiße' [bair-leen-er vice-uh], a kind of shandy.

**lake** der See [zay]
**lamb** das Lamm
**lamp** die Lampe [lamp-uh]
**lamppost** der Laternenpfahl [latairnen-pfahl]
**lampshade** der Lampenschirm [-sheerm]
**land** das Land [lant]
**lane** *(on road)* die Spur [shpoor]
**langsam fahren** drive slowly
**language** die Sprache [shprahкнuh]
**language course** ein Sprachkurs [shprahкн-koorss]
**laptop** ein Laptop [lep-top]
**large** groß [grohss]
**laryngitis** die Kehlkopfentzündung [kayl-kopf-ent-tsœn-doong]
**last** letzter [lets-ter]
  **last year** letztes Jahr
  **last week** letzte Woche [...vокн-uh]
  **last night** gestern Abend [ghestairn ah-bent]

*(during the night)* gestern Nacht [...nahкнт]
  **at last!** endlich! [ent-lisн]
**late** spät [shpayt]
  **sorry I'm late** entschuldigen Sie, dass ich zu
  spät komme [ent-shool-dig-en zee dass isн tsoo
  shpayt kommuh]
  **it's a bit late** es ist ein bisschen spät [...bis-
  sнen...]
  **please hurry, I'm late** bitte beeilen Sie sich, ich
  bin spät dran [bittuh buh-ı-len zee zisн isн bin
  shpayt dran]
  **at the latest** spätestens [shpayt-ess-tenz]
**later** später [shpayter]
  **see you later** bis später!
**laugh** *(verb)* lachen [lah◆кнen]
**launderette** der Waschsalon [vash-salong]

> ✈ Not that common. Try a **Sofortreinigung**
> instead (fast-service dry-cleaner's).

**lavatory** die Toilette [twalet-uh]
**law** das Gesetz [gheh-zets]
**Lawinengefahr** danger of avalanches
**lawyer** der Rechtsanwalt [resнts-anvalt]
  *(woman)* die Rechtsanwältin [-anveltin]
**laxative** ein Abführmittel [ap-foor-mittel]
**lazy** faul [fowl]
**leaf** das Blatt
**leak** eine undichte Stelle [oon-disн-tuh shtel-uh]
  **it leaks** es ist nicht dicht
**learn: I want to learn...** ich möchte...lernen [isн
  mursнtuh...lair-nen]
**lease** *(verb)* mieten [meeten]
  *(land, premises)* pachten [paкн-ten]
**least: not in the least** nicht im Geringsten [nisнt
  im gheringsten]
  **at least** mindestens [min-dess-tenz]
**leather** das Leder [lay-der]

**leave: we're leaving tomorrow** wir *fahren* morgen *ab* [veer faren...ap]

**when does the bus leave?** wann fährt der Bus? [van fairt dair booss]

**I left two shirts in my room** ich habe zwei Hemden in meinem Zimmer *liegen lassen* [iSH hah-buh tsvy...lee-ghen...]

**can I leave this here?** kann ich das hier lassen?

**Lebensgefahr** danger

**left** linke [link-uh]

**on the left** links

**left-handed: to be left-handed** Linkshänder sein [links-hender zine]

**left luggage (office)** die Gepäckaufbewahrung [gheh-peck-owf-buh-varoong]

**leg** das Bein [bine]

**legal** *(permitted)* legal [lay-gahl]

**lemon** eine Zitrone [tsitro-nuh]

**lemonade** eine Limonade [leemo-na-duh]

**lend: will you lend me your...?** leihen Sie mir Ihr...? [ly-en zee meer eer]

**lens** *(for camera)* das Objektiv [op-yek-teef]

*(of glasses)* das Glas [glahss]

**less** weniger [vay-nee-gher]

**let: let me help** kann ich helfen?

**let me go!** lassen Sie mich los! [...lohss]

**will you let me off here?** würden Sie mich hier aussteigen lassen? [voorden zee misH heer owss-shty-ghen...]

**let's go** gehen wir! [gay-en veer]

**letter** der Brief [breef]

*(of alphabet)* der Buchstabe [bookH-shtahb-uh]

**are there any letters for me?** habe ich Post? [hah-buh isH posst]

**letterbox** der Briefkasten [breefkasten]

✈ Letterboxes are yellow.

**lettuce** der Kopfsalat [kopf-zalaht]
**level-crossing** der Bahnübergang [bahn-ōober-gang]
**liable** *(responsible)* haftbar
**library** die Bibliothek [bee-blee-o-tayk]
**licence** die Genehmigung [gheh-naym-igoong]
    *(driving)* der Führerschein [fōorer-shine]
**lid** der Deckel
**lie** *(untruth)* eine Lüge [lōog-uh]
   **can he lie down for a bit?** kann er sich ein bisschen hinlegen? [kan air zisн ine bis-sнen hin-lay-ghen]
**life** das Leben [lay-ben]
   **that's life** so ist das Leben [zo...]
**lifebelt** der Rettungsgürtel [ret-oongs-gōortel]
**lifeboat** das Rettungsboot [ret-oongs-boht]
**life-guard** der Bademeister [bah-duh-my-ster]
   *(woman)* die Bademeisterin
   *(on beach)* der Rettungsschwimmer [ret-oongs-shvimmer]
   *(woman)* die Rettungsschwimmerin
**life insurance** eine Lebensversicherung [lay-benz-fair-zisн-eroong]
**life jacket** eine Schwimmweste [shvim-vest-uh]
**lift: do you want a lift?** kann ich Sie mitnehmen? [kan isн zee mit-nay-men]
   **could you give me a lift?** könnten Sie mich mitnehmen? [kurnten zee...]
   **the lift isn't working** der *Fahrstuhl* ist außer Betrieb [...fahr-shtool ist owsser buh-treep]
**light** *(not heavy)* leicht [lysнt]
   *(not dark)* hell
   **the light** das Licht [lisнt]
   **the lights aren't working** das Licht geht nicht [...gayt nisнt]
   *(of car)* die Scheinwerfer funktionieren nicht [shine-vairfer foonk-tsee-ohn-ee-ren...]

**have you got a light?** haben Sie Feuer? [hah-ben zee foy-er]

**light blue** hellblau

**light bulb** die Glühbirne [gloo-beern-uh]

**lighter** ein Feuerzeug [foy-er-tsoyg]

**like: would you like…?** möchten Sie…? [mursHten zee]

**I'd like a…** ich hätte gerne ein… [isH het-uh gairn-uh ine]

**I'd like to…** ich würde gerne… [voorduh…]

**I like it** das gefällt mir [dass gheh-felt meer]

**I like you** ich mag Sie/dich gern *(polite/familiar)* [isH mahg zee/disH gairn]

**I don't like it** das gefällt mir nicht […nisHt]

**what's it like?** wie ist es? [vee…]

**like yours** wie deins

**do it like this** machen Sie es so [mahkHen zee ess zo]

**one like that** so einer [zo ine-er]

**lime** eine Limone [leemo-nuh]

**lime juice** ein Limonensaft [leemohn-en-zaft]

**line** die Linie [lee-nee-uh]

*(telephone)* die Leitung [ly-toong]

**links** left

**lip** die Lippe [lip-uh]

**lip salve** ein Fettlippenstift [-shtift]

**lipstick** der Lippenstift [-shtift]

**liqueur** ein Likör [lik-ur]

**list** die Liste [list-uh]

**listen** zuhören [tsoo-hur-ren]

**listen!** hören Sie zu! [hur-ren zee tsoo]

**litre** der Liter [leeter]

✈ 1 litre = 1.75 pints = 0.22 gals

**little** klein [kline]

**a little ice** ein wenig Eis [ine vaynisH ice]

**a little more** noch ein wenig [noKH…]

**just a little** nur ein wenig, nur ein bisschen [noor...bis-sHen]

**live** wohnen [vo-nen]

*(be alive)* leben [lay-ben]

**I live in Glasgow** ich wohne in Glasgow [isH vo-nuh...]

**where do you live?** wo wohnen Sie? [vo...zee]

**liver** die Leber [lay-ber]

**Lkw, Lastkraftwagen** lorry, truck

**loaf** ein Brot [broht]

**lobster** ein Hummer [hoomer]

**local: could we try a local wine?** könnten wir einen Wein *aus der Gegend* probieren? [kumten veer ine-en vine owss dair gay-ghent pro-beeren]

**a local restaurant** ein Restaurant im Ort [...restor-rong...]

**lock: the lock's broken** das Schloss ist kaputt [...shloss...]

**I've locked myself out** ich habe mich ausgeschlossen [isH hah-buh misH owss-gheh-shlossen]

**lonely** einsam [ine-zahm]

**long** lang

**we'd like to stay longer** wir würden gerne etwas länger bleiben [veer voorden gairn-uh etvass leng-er bly-ben]

**a long time** lange [lang-uh]

**loo: where's the loo?** wo ist das Klo? [vo...]

**look: you look tired** Sie *sehen* müde *aus* [zee zay-en mood-uh owss]

**look at that** schauen Sie sich das an [showen zee zisH...]

**can I have a look?** kann ich mal sehen? [...zay-en]

**I'm just looking** ich will mich nur umsehen [isH vil misH noor oom-zay-en]

**will you look after my bags?** passt du auf

meine Taschen auf? [...owf mine-uh tashen owf]

**I'm looking for...** ich suche... [ish zooКН-uh]

**look out!** Vorsicht! [for-zisHt]

**loose** lose [lo-zuh]

*(clothes)* locker

**lorry** der Lastwagen [lasst-vah-ghen]

**lorry driver** der Lkw-Fahrer [el-kah-vay-farer]

**lose** verlieren [fair-leer-ren]

**I've lost...** ich habe...verloren [ish hah-buh...
fair-lor-ren]

**excuse me, I'm lost** entschuldigen Sie, ich
habe mich verlaufen [ent-shool-dig-en zee ish
hah-buh mish fair-lowf-en]

*(driving)* ich habe mich verfahren [...fair-faren]

**lost property (office)** das Fundbüro [foont-bōō-
ro]

**lot: a lot** viel [feel]

**not a lot** nicht viel [nisHt...]

**a lot of chips** eine Menge Pommes frites [ine-
uh meng-uh pom frit]

**a lot of wine** viel Wein [...vine]

**a lot more expensive** viel teurer [...toy-rer]

**lotion** die Lotion [lohts-ee-ohn]

**loud** *(noise)* laut [lowt]

**louder** lauter [lowter]

**it's too loud** es ist zu laut [...tsoo...]

**lounge** *(in house)* das Wohnzimmer [vohn-
tsimmer]

*(in hotel)* die Lounge

*(at airport)* der Warteraum [vart-uh-rowm]

**love: I love you** ich liebe dich [ish leebuh dish]

**do you love me?** liebst du mich? [leepst doo
mish]

**he/she's in love** er/sie ist verliebt [air/zee ist fair-
leept]

**I love this wine** ich mag diesen Wein sehr [ish
mahg dee-zen vine zair]

**lovely** schön [shurn]
**low** niedrig [nee-drisн]
**luck** das Glück [glōck]
  **good luck!** viel Glück! [feel...]
**lucky** Glücks- [glōcks-]
  **you're lucky** Sie haben Glück [zee hah-ben...]
  **that's lucky!** Glück gehabt! [...geh-hahpt]
**luggage** das Gepäck [gheh-peck]
**lunch** das Mittagessen [mitahg-essen]
**lungs** die Lungen [loong-en]
**luxury** der Luxus [looks-ooss]

# M [em]

**mad** verrückt [fair-rōckt]
**made-to-measure** nach Maß [nahкн mahss]
**magazine** eine Zeitschrift [site-shrift]
**magnificent** großartig [grohss-artisн]
**maid** das Zimmermädchen [tsimmer-mayd-sнen]
**maiden name** der Mädchenname [mayd-sнen-nah-muh]
**mail** die Post [posst]
  **is there any mail for me?** habe ich Post? [hah-buh isн...]
**main road** die Hauptstraße [howpt-shtrass-uh]
**make** machen [mahкнen]
  **will we make it in time?** schaffen wir das rechtzeitig? [shaffen veer dass resнt-tsite-isн]
**make-up** das 'Make-up'
**man** der Mann
**manager** der Geschäftsführer [gheh-shefts-fōōr-er]
  *(woman)* die Geschäftsführerin
  **can I see the manager?** kann ich mit dem Geschäftsführer sprechen? [...shpresнen]
**many** viele [feel-uh]
**map** die Karte [kartuh]
  *(of city)* ein Stadtplan [shtat-plahn]

**a map of Munich** ein Stadtplan von München

**March** März [mairts]

**marina** der Jachthafen [yaкнt-hah-fen]

**market** der Markt

**marmalade** die Orangenmarmelade [oron-Jen-marmuh-lah-duh]

**married** verheiratet [fair-hy-raht-et]

**marry: will you marry me?** willst du mich heiraten? [vilst doo misн hy-raht-en]

**marvellous** wunderbar [voonderbar]

**mascara** die Wimperntusche [vimpern-toosh-uh]

**mashed potatoes** der Kartoffelbrei [kartoffel-bry]

**mass** (in church) die Messe [mess-uh]

**massage** eine Massage [massah-Juh]

**mast** der Mast [masst]

**mat** die Matte [mat-uh]

**match: a box of matches** eine Schachtel Streichhölzer [shaкнtel shtrysн-hurltser]

**a football match** ein Fußballspiel [fooss-bal-shpeel]

**material** (cloth) das Material [ma-tay-ree-ahl]

**matter: it doesn't matter** das macht nichts [dass mahкнt nisнts]

**what's the matter?** was ist los? [vass ist lohss]

**mattress** die Matratze [ma-trats-uh]

**mature** reif [rife]

**maximum** das Maximum [maksimoom]

**May** Mai [my]

**may: may I have...?** darf ich...haben? [...isн...hah-ben]

**maybe** vielleicht [fee-lysнt]

**mayonnaise** die Mayonnaise [my-on-ay-zuh]

**me: he knows me** er kennt *mich* [...misн]

**give it to me** geben Sie es *mir* [...meer]

**for me** für mich

**with/from me** mit/von mir [...fon...]

**it's me** ich bin's [isн...]

**it was me** ich war es [iSH var ess]

**who? – me** wer? – ich

**meal** das Essen

**mean: what does this mean?** was heißt das?
[vass hysst dass]

**measles** die Masern [mah-zern]

**German measles** die Röteln [rur-teln]

**measurements** die Maße [mahss-uh]

**meat** das Fleisch [flysh]

**mechanic: is there a mechanic here?** gibt es
hier einen Mechaniker? [gheept ess heer ine-en
meSH-ahn-iker]

**medicine** die Medizin [medi-tseen]

**Mediterranean** das Mittelmeer [mittel-mayr]

**meet** treffen

**pleased to meet you** angenehm! [an-gheh-
naym]

**meeting** die Besprechung [buh-shpreSH-∞ng]

**melon** eine Melone [melo-nuh]

**member** das Mitglied [mit-gleet]

**how do I become a member?** wie werde ich
Mitglied? [vee vair-duh iSH...]

**men** Männer [men-er]

**mend: can you mend this?** können Sie das
reparieren? [kurnen zee dass rep-a-ree-ren]
*(clothes)* können Sie das flicken?

**mention: don't mention it** gern geschehen
[gairn gheh-shay-en]

**menu** die Speisekarte [shpy-zuh-kartuh]

**can I have the menu, please?** kann ich bitte
die Speisekarte haben?
*go to pages 84-87*

**mess** ein Durcheinander [d∞rSH-ine-ander]

**message** die Nachricht [nahKH-risHt]
*(text)* eine SMS [ess-em-ess]

**are there any messages for me?** hat jemand
eine Nachricht für mich hinterlassen? [...yay-

mant ine-uh...foor misH...]
**can I leave a message for...?** kann ich eine
Nachricht für...hinterlassen?
**metre** der Meter [may-ter]

✈ 1 metre = 39.37 inches = 1.09 yds

**midday** der Mittag [mitahg]
  **at midday** mittags
**middle** die Mitte [mit-uh]
  **in the middle** in der Mitte [in dair...]
**midnight** Mitternacht [miter-nahkHt]
**might: he might have gone** er ist *vielleicht*
  schon gegangen [air ist fee-lysht shohn gheh-
  gang-en]
**migraine** eine Migräne [mee-grayn-uh]
**mild** mild [milt]
**mile** die Meile [my-luh]

✈ miles/5 x 8 = kilometres

| miles | 0.5 | 1 | 3 | 5 | 10 | 50 | 100 |
|---|---|---|---|---|---|---|---|
| kilometres | 0.8 | 1.6 | 4.8 | 8 | 16 | 80 | 160 |

**milk** die Milch [milsH]
  **a glass of milk** ein Glas Milch
**milkshake** das Milchmixgetränk [milsH-miks-gheh-
  trenk]
**millimetre** der Millimeter [mili-mayter]
**milometer** der Kilometerzähler [kilo-mayter-tsayler]
**mind: I've changed my mind** ich habe es mir
  anders überlegt [isH hah-buh ess meer anders
  ööberlaygt]
  **I don't mind** das macht mir nichts aus [dass
  mahkHt meer nisHts owss]
  **I don't mind** *(it's all the same)* es ist mir egal
  [...ay-gahl]
  **do you mind if I...?** macht es Ihnen etwas aus,
  wenn ich... [mahkHt ess ee-nen etvass owss ven isH]
  **never mind** macht nichts [mahkHt nisHts]

**I'd like**
ich hätte
gern
[...het-uh
gairn]

## Vorspeisen: Starters

**Gänseleberpastete** goose liver pâté
**Gemischte Meeresfrüchte** selection of seafood
**Knoblauchbrot** garlic bread
**Königinpastete** chicken vol-au-vent
**Krabbencocktail** prawn cocktail
**Muscheln** mussels
**Russische Eier** eggs mayonnaise
**Weinbergschnecken** snails

## Suppen: Soups

**Hühnerbrühe** chicken broth
**Kraftbrühe** beef consommé
**Leberknödelsuppe** liver dumpling soup
**Ochsenschwanzsuppe** oxtail soup
**Spargelcremesuppe** cream of asparagus soup
**Tagessuppe** soup of the day
**Zwiebelsuppe** onion soup

**water**
Wasser

**bread**
Brot
[broht]

## Vom Rind: Beef

**Deutsches Beefsteak** mince patty
**Falscher Hase** meat loaf
**Frikadelle** rissole
**Rinderbraten** pot roast
**Rinderfilet** fillet steak
**Rinderzunge** ox tongue
**Rostbraten** steak with onions
**Roulade** beef olive
**Sauerbraten** marinaded potroast
**Tatar** raw mince with spices

**beef**
Rindfleisch

**chicken**
Hähnchen
[haynsHen]

**lamb**
Lamm

## Vom Schwein: Pork

**Eisbein** boiled knuckle of pork
**Kassler** smoked and braised pork chops
**Schweinebauch** belly of pork
**Schweinebraten** roast pork
**Schweinekotelett** pork chop
**Schweinerippe** cured pork chop

**Schweineschnitzel** pork fillet
**Schweinshaxe** knuckle of pork

### Geflügel: Poultry

**Brathähnchen** roast chicken
**Entenbraten** roast duck
**Gänsebraten** roast goose
**Putenschnitzel** turkey escalope

### Vom Kalb: Veal

**Gefüllte Kalbsbrust** stuffed breast of veal
**Holsteiner Schnitzel** breaded veal cutlet with vegetables and a fried egg
**Jägerschnitzel** veal with mushrooms
**Kalbshaxe** knuckle of veal
**Kalbsnierenbraten** roast veal with kidneys
**Wiener Schnitzel** veal in breadcrumbs
**Zigeunerschnitzel** veal or pork with peppers and relishes

### Wild: Game

**Fasan** pheasant
**Hasenbraten** roast hare
**Rehbraten** roast venison
**Wildschweinsteak** wild boar steak

### Fischgerichte: Fish

**Forelle Müllerin (Art)** trout dipped in flour and butter and served with lemon
**Lachs** salmon
**Matjesheringe** pickled herrings
**Seezunge** sole

### Spezialitäten: Specialities

**Bauernfrühstück** scrambled eggs with potatoes and bacon
**Fleischkäse** meat loaf
**Geselchtes** salted and smoked meat

---

**can I have what he's having?**
ich hätte gern das Gleiche wie er
[...glySHuh vee air]

---

**red wine**
Rotwein
[roht-vine]

**white wine**
Weißwein
[vice-vine]

**beer**
Bier

**Geschnetzeltes** meat cut into strips in creamy sauce
**Kohl und Pinkel** cabbage, potatoes, sausage and smoked meat
**Königsberger Klopse** meatballs in caper sauce
**Labskaus** meat, fish and potato stew
**Leberkäse** baked pork and beef loaf
**Maultaschen** pasta filled with meat, vegetables or cheese
**Schlachtplatte** selection of sausages and meat
**Sülze** brawn
**Tafelspitz** soured boiled rump of beef
**Wurstplatte** selection of cold sausages

### Beilagen: Vegetables etc

**Blumenkohl** cauliflower
**Bratkartoffeln** fried potatoes
**Erbsen** peas
**Feldsalat** lamb's lettuce
**Gemüse** vegetable(s)
**Gemüseplatte** assorted vegetables
**Grüne Bohnen** French beans
**Kartoffelbrei** mashed potatoes
**Klöße** dumplings
**Knödel** dumplings
**Kohl** cabbage
**Lauch** leek
**Nudeln** noodles
**Pfifferlinge** chanterelles
**Pilze** mushrooms
**Pommes frites** French fries
**Rohkostplatte** selection of salads
**Rosenkohl** Brussels sprouts
**Röstkartoffeln** fried potatoes
**Rotkraut** red cabbage
**Salatteller** side salad; selection of salads
**Salzkartoffeln** boiled potatoes

very nice
sehr gut

**Sauerkraut** white cabbage, finely chopped and pickled
**Semmelknödel** bread dumplings
**Spargel** asparagus
**Spätzle** home-made noodles
**Spinat** spinach
**Teigwaren** pasta
**Wirsing** savoy cabbage

## Snacks: Snacks

**Bockwurst** large Frankfurter sausage
**Bratwurst** grilled pork sausage
**Halbes Hähnchen** half a (roast) chicken
**Käsebrot** bread and cheese
**Schinkenbrot** bread and ham (often raw)

## Nachspeisen: Desserts

**Apfelstrudel** apple strudel
**Birne Helene** pear with chocolate sauce
**Eis** ice; ice cream
**Eisbecher mit Sahne** sundae with cream
**Obstsalat** fruit salad
**Rote Grütze** red fruit jelly
**Sachertorte** rich chocolate cake
**Schwarzwälder Kirschtorte** Black Forest cherry gateau

## General Terms

**Bedienung inbegriffen** service included
**Gedeck** set meal
**Hausmacher (Art)** home-made style
**Kinderteller** children's portion
**Nach Art des Hauses** à la maison
**Nach Hausfrauenart** home-made
**Seniorenteller** smaller, cheaper dish for OAPs
**Tageskarte** menu of the day

vanilla
Vanille

strawberry
Erdbeer

chocolate
Schokolade

coffee
ein Kaffee

the bill, please
zahlen, bitte

**mine** meiner/meine/meins [mine-er/mine-uh/mine-ss]

> These forms correspond to the articles **der/die/das**. The plural is **meine**.

**mineral water** ein Mineralwasser [minerahl-vasser]

**minimum** das Minimum [minimoom]

**minus** minus [mee-nooss]
  **minus 3 degrees** drei Grad minus [...graht...]

**minute** die Minute [minoot-uh]
  **in a minute** gleich [glysH]
  **just a minute** einen Moment, bitte [ine-en moment bittuh]

**mirror** der Spiegel [shpee-ghel]

**Miss** Fräulein [froy-line]

**miss: I miss you** du fehlst mir [doo faylst meer]
  **he's missing** er ist verschwunden [air ist fair-shvoonden]
  **there is a...missing** da fehlt ein... [da faylt ine]
  **we missed the bus** wir haben den Bus verpasst [veer hah-ben dayn booss fair-passt]

**mist** der Nebel [naybel]

**mistake** ein Fehler [fayler]
  **I think you've made a mistake** ich glaube, Sie haben sich vertan [isH glow-buh zee hah-ben zisH fair-tahn]

**misunderstanding** ein Missverständnis [miss-fair-shtent-niss]

**mobile (phone)** ein Handy [hendee]
  **my mobile number is...** meine Handynummer ist... [mine-uh hendee-noommer...]

**modern** modern [modairn]

**moisturizer** eine Feuchtigkeitscreme [foysHtisH-kites-kraym]

**Monday** Montag [mohntahg]

**money** das Geld [ghelt]

**I've lost my money** ich habe mein Geld
verloren [isH hah-buh mine ghelt fair-lor-ren]
**I have no money** ich habe kein Geld
[...kine...]
**money belt** eine Gürteltasche [goortel-tash-uh]
**month** der Monat [mo-naht]
**moon** der Mond [mohnt]
**moped** das Moped
**more** mehr [mair]
   **can I have some more?** kann ich noch etwas
   haben? [kan isH nokH etvass hah-ben]
   **more bread, please** noch etwas Brot, bitte
   [nokH etvass broht bittuh]
   **no more thanks** danke, das reicht [dank-uh dass
   rysHt]
   **no more money** kein Geld mehr [kine...mair]
   **more than...** mehr als... [...alss]
   **there aren't any more** es sind keine mehr da
   **more comfortable** bequemer [buh-kvaymer]
**morning** der Morgen [mor-ghen]
   **good morning** guten Morgen [gooten...]
   **in the morning** morgens [morghenz]
   *(tomorrow)* morgen früh [...froo]
   **this morning** heute Morgen [hoytuh...]
**most: I like this one the most** das gefällt mir am
   besten [gheh-felt meer...]
   **most of the people** die meisten Leute [dee my-
   sten loytuh]
**mother: my mother** meine Mutter [mine-uh
   mooter]
**motor** der Motor [mo-tor]
**motorbike** das Motorrad [mo-tor-raht]
**motorcyclist** der Motorradfahrer [mo-tor-raht-
   farer]
   *(woman)* die Motorradfahrerin
**motorist** der Autofahrer [owto-farer]
   *(woman)* die Autofahrerin

**motorway** die Autobahn [owto-bahn]
**mountain** der Berg [bairk]
  **in the mountains** in den Bergen [in dayn bairghen]
**mountaineer** ein Bergsteiger [bairk-shtyger]
  *(woman)* eine Bergsteigerin
**mountaineering** das Bergsteigen [bairk-shtygen]
**mouse** *(also for computer)* die Maus [mowss]
**moustache** ein Schnurrbart [shnoor-bart]
**mouth** der Mund [moont]
**move: don't move** bewegen Sie sich nicht! [buh-vay-ghen zee ziSH nisHt]
  **could you move your car?** könnten Sie Ihren Wagen wegfahren? [kurnten zee eer-en vah-ghen vek-faren]
**movie** der Film
**MPV** ein Van
**Mr** Herr [hair]
**Mrs** Frau [frow]
**Ms** Frau [frow]
**much** viel [feel]
  **much better** viel besser
  **not much** nicht viel [nisHt...]
**mug: I've been mugged** ich bin *überfallen* worden [isH bin ōōber-fal-en vorden]
**mum: my mum** meine Mutter [mine-uh mooter]
**muscle** der Muskel [mooskel]
**museum** das Museum [moo-zay-ōōm]

  ✈ Most museums close on Mondays.

**mushrooms** Pilze [pilts-uh]
**music** die Musik [moozeek]
**must: I must have...** ich muss...haben [isH mooss...hah-ben]
  **you must do it** Sie müssen es tun [zee mōōssen ess toon]
  **I must not eat...** ich darf...nicht essen [isH

darf...nisHt...]

> Be careful with the negative.
> **you mustn't...** du darfst nicht...
> *(polite form)* Sie dürfen nicht...
>
> If you say **du musst nicht...** or **Sie müssen nicht...** that means 'you don't have to...' and not 'you must not...'

**mustard** der Senf [zenf]
**MWSt, Mehrwertsteuer** VAT
**my** mein/meine/mein [mine/mine-uh...]

> These forms correspond to the articles
> **der/die/das**. The plural is **meine**.
> **my husband/wife** mein Mann/
> meine Frau

# N [en]

**nail** *(on finger, for wood)* der Nagel [nah-ghel]
**nail clippers** der Nagelknipser [nah-ghel-kuh-nips-er]
**nail file** eine Nagelfeile [nah-ghel-fy-luh]
**nail polish** der Nagellack [nah-ghel-lack]
**nail scissors** die Nagelschere [nah-ghel-shay-ruh]
**naked** nackt
**name** der Name [nah-muh]
  **my name is...** ich heiße... [isH hice-uh]
  **what's your name?** wie heißen Sie? [vee hice-en zee]
  *(familiar)* wie heißt du? [...hyst doo]
**napkin** die Serviette [zair-vee-ettuh]
**nappy** die Windel [vindel]
**narrow** eng
**national** national [natsee-o-nahl]

**nationality** die Nationalität [natsee-o-nahl-ee-tayt]

**natural** natürlich [natöorlisн]

**naughty: don't be naughty** sei nicht frech [zy nisнt fresн]

**near: is it near?** ist es in der Nähe? [ist ess in dair nay-uh]

    **near here** hier herum [heer hairoom]

    **do you go near…?** kommen Sie in die Nähe von…? […zee in dee nay-uh fon]

    **where's the nearest …?** wo ist der/die/das nächste…? [vo ist dair/dee/dass neks-stuh]

**nearly** fast [fasst]

**neat** *(drink)* pur [poor]

**necessary** notwendig [noht-vendisн]

    **it's not necessary** das ist nicht notwendig

**neck** der Hals [halss]

**necklace** die Halskette [halss-ket-uh]

**need: I need a…** ich brauche einen… [isн browкн-uh ine-en]

**needle** die Nadel [nah-del]

**neighbour** der Nachbar [nahкн-bar]
    *(woman)* die Nachbarin

**neither: neither of them** keiner/keine von beiden [kine-er/kine-uh fon by-den]

    **neither…nor…** weder…noch… [vayder… noкн…]

    **neither am/do I** ich auch nicht [isн owкн nisнt]

**nephew: my nephew** mein Neffe [mine nef-uh]

**nervous** nervös [nair-vurss]

**net** *(sport, fishing)* das Netz

**never** niemals [nee-malss]

**new** neu [noy]

**news** die Nachrichten [nahкн-risнten]

**newsagent's** ein Zeitungshändler [tsytoongs-hendler]

**newspaper** die Zeitung [tsytoong]
  **do you have any English newspapers?** haben
  Sie englische Zeitungen? [hah-ben zee eng-lish-
  uh tsytoong-en]
**New Year** Neujahr [noy-yar]
  **Happy New Year** ein gutes neues Jahr! [ine
  gootess noy-ess yar]

> ✈ New Year is celebrated with fireworks
> and, traditionally, champagne at midnight
> when people say **Prost Neujahr** [prohst
> noy-yahr]. You can wish someone **guten
> Rutsch** [gooten...] when you say goodbye
> to them just before New Year.

**New Year's Eve** Silvester
**New Zealand** Neuseeland [noy-zay-lant]
**next** nächste [nekstuh]
  **please stop at the next corner** halten Sie
  bitte an der nächsten Ecke [...zee bittuh an dair
  neksten eckuh]
  **see you next year** bis nächstes Jahr [biss
  nekstess yar]
  **next week/next Tuesday** nächste Woche/
  nächsten Dienstag
  **next to the hotel** neben dem Hotel [nay-ben
  daym...]
**next of kin** der/die nächste Angehörige [nekstuh
  an-gheh-hur-iguh]
**nice** schön [shurn]
  *(person)* nett
  *(nice-looking)* hübsch [hoopsh]
  *(pleasant, kind)* sympathisch [zoompahtish]
  *(food)* lecker
**nicht berühren** do not touch
**nicht öffnen** do not open
**Nichtraucher** no smoking
**niece: my niece** meine Nichte [mine-uh nisHt-uh]

**night** die Nacht [nahкнt]
  **good night** gute Nacht [gootuh...]
  **at night** nachts [nahкнts]
**night club** ein Nachtklub [nahкнt-klɔob ]
**nightdress** ein Nachthemd [nahкнt-hemt]
**night porter** der Nachtportier [nahкнt-por-tee-ay]
**no** nein [nine]
  **we have no water** wir haben *kein* Wasser [veer
  hah-ben kine vasser]
  **there are no...** es gibt keine... [...kine-uh]
**nobody** niemand [nee-mant]
  **nobody saw it** *keiner* hat es gesehen [kine-er
  hat ess gheh-zay-en]
**noisy** laut [lowt]
  **our room is too noisy** in unserem Zimmer ist
  es zu laut [in ɔonzerem tsimmer ist ess tsoo...]
**none** keine [kine-uh]
**non-smoker: we're non-smokers** wir sind
  Nichtraucher [veer zint nisнt-rowkнer]
**nor: nor am/do I** ich auch nicht [isн owkн nisнt]
**normal** normal [normahl]
**north** der Norden
**Northern Ireland** Nordirland [nort-eer-lant]
**nose** die Nase [nah-zuh]
**not** nicht [nisнt]
  **not that one** das nicht [dass...]
  **not me** ich nicht [isн...]
  **I don't want to...** ich will nicht... [...vil...]
  **he didn't tell me** er hat mir das nicht gesagt
  [air hat meer dass nisнt gheh-zahgt]
**Notausgang** emergency exit
**Notausstieg** emergency exit
**Notbremse** emergency brake
**note** *(bank note)* der Schein [shine]
**nothing** nichts [nisнts]
**November** November
**now** jetzt [yetst]

**nowhere** nirgends [neer-ghents]
**nudist beach** ein FKK-Strand [ef-ka-ka-shtrant]
**nuisance: it's a nuisance** das ist ärgerlich [dass ist air-gher-lish]
  **this man's being a nuisance** der Mann belästigt mich [...buh-lest-isht mish]
**numb** taub [towp]
**number** *(figure)* die Zahl [tsahl]
**number plate** das Nummernschild [noomern-shilt]
**nur für Anlieger** residents only
**nurse** die Krankenschwester [kranken-shvester]
  *(male)* der Krankenpfleger [kranken-pflay-gher]
**nursery slope** der Idiotenhügel [id-ee-o-ten-hoo-ghel]
**nut** die Nuss [nooss]
  *(on bolt)* die Schraubenmutter [shrowben-mooter]

# O [oh]

**oar** das Ruder [rooder]
**obligatory** obligatorisch [obleegator-rish]
**obviously** offensichtlich [offen-zisht-lish]
**occasionally** gelegentlich [gheh-lay-ghent-lish]
**o'clock** *go to* **time**
**October** Oktober
**odd** *(number)* ungerade [oon-gheh-rah-duh]
  *(strange)* seltsam [zelt-zahm]
**of** von [fon]

> To express 'of' you can also change the words **der/die/das** to **des/der/des**. With **des** you add an **-s** to the following noun.
>   **the name of the hotel** der Name des Hotels
> Here **das Hotel** becomes **des Hotels**.

> **the name of the street** der Name der
> Straße
> Here **die Straße** becomes **der Straße**.

**off: the milk is off** die Milch ist sauer [dee milsн
ist zow-er]
   **the meat is off** das Fleisch ist schlecht [dass
flysh ist shlesнt]
   **it just came off** es ist einfach abgegangen
   [...ine-fahкн ap-gheh-gang-en]
   **10% off** 10% Ermäßigung [tsayn pro-tsent air-
mace-igœng]
**office** das Büro [bōōro]
**official** der Beamte [buh-am-tuh]
   *(woman)* die Beamtin
**Öffnungszeiten** opening hours
**often** oft
   **how often?** wie oft? [vee...]
   **not often** nicht oft [nisнt...]
   **how often do the buses go?** wie oft fährt der
Bus? [...fairt...]

> *YOU MAY THEN HEAR*
> alle zehn Minuten *every ten minutes*
> zweimal pro Stunde *twice an hour*

**oil** das Öl [url]
   **will you change the oil?** könnten Sie bitte das
Öl wechseln? [kurnten zee bittuh dass url vekseln]
**ointment** eine Salbe [zalb-uh]
**ok** 'okay'
   **it's ok** *(doesn't matter)* das ist in Ordnung
   [...ordnœng]
   **are you ok?** alles in Ordnung? [al-ess...]
   **that's ok by me** von mir aus ist das in Ordnung
   [fon meer owss ist dass...]
   **is this ok for the airport?** *(bus, train)* geht der
zum Flughafen? [gayt dair tsœm...]

**more wine? – no, I'm ok thanks** noch Wein?
– nein, danke [noкн vine – nine dank-uh]
**old** alt [al-t]
  **how old are you?** wie alt bist du? [vee…doo]

> **I am 28** ich bin 28

**olive** die Olive [o-lee-vuh]
**omelette** ein Omelett [omlet]
**on** auf [owf]
  **I haven't got it on me** ich habe es nicht bei
  mir [ish hah-buh ess nisht by meer]
  **on Friday** am Freitag [am fry-tahg]
  **on television** im Fernsehen [im fairn-zay-en]
**once** einmal [ine-mahl]
  **at once** (immediately) sofort [zo-fort]
**one** ein/eine/ein [ine/ine-uh…]
  (number) eins [ine-ss]
  **the red one** der/die/das rote [dair/dee/dass ro-
  tuh]
**onion** die Zwiebel [tsveebel]
**on-line: to pay on-line** 'online' bezahlen […buh-
  tsahlen]
**only** nur [noor]
  **the only one** der/die/das einzige [dair ine-tsig-
  uh]
**open** (adjective) offen
  **I can't open it** ich bekomme es nicht auf [ish
  buh-kommuh ess nisht owf]
  **when do you open?** wann machen Sie auf?
  [van mahкнen zee owf]
**open ticket** ein offenes Ticket
**opera** die Oper [o-per]
**operation** die Operation [o-per-ats-ee-ohn]
**operator** (telephone) die Vermittlung [fair-
  mitloong]
**opposite: opposite the hotel** gegenüber dem
  Hotel [gay-ghen-ööber daym…]

**optician's** der Optiker

**or** oder [o-der]

**orange** *(fruit)* eine Orange [oronJuh]
  *(colour)* orange [oronJ]

**orange juice** der Orangensaft [oronJen-zaft]

**order: could we order now?** könnten wir jetzt
  *bestellen*? [kurnten veer yetst buh-shtellen]
  **thank you, we've already ordered** danke,
  wir haben schon bestellt [dankuh veer hah-ben
  shohn buh-shtelt]

**other: the other one** der/die/das andere [dair/
  dee/dass an-der-uh]
  **do you have any others?** haben Sie
  irgendwelche andere? [hah-ben zee eergent-
  velsh-uh an-der-uh]

**otherwise** sonst [z-]

**ought: I ought to go** ich *sollte* gehen [isH zolt-uh
  gay-en]

**our** unser/unsere/unser [oon-zer/oon-zuh-ruh...]

**ours** unserer/unsere/unseres [oon-zuh-rer/oon-zuh-
  ruh/oon-zuh-ress]

---

> These forms correspond to the articles
> **der/die/das**. The plural is **unsere**.

---

**out: we're out of petrol** uns ist das Benzin
  ausgegangen [oonss ist dass ben-tseen owss-
  gheh-gang-en]
  **get out!** raus! [rowss]

**outdoors** im Freien [im fry-en]

**outside: can we sit outside?** können wir *draußen*
  sitzen? [kurnen veer drowssen zitsen]

**over: over here** hier drüben [heer drooben]
  **over there** dort drüben
  **over 40** über vierzig [oober...]
  **it's all over** *(finished)* es ist aus [ess ist owss]

**overcharge: you've overcharged me** Sie haben
  mir *zu viel berechnet* [zee hah-ben meer tsoo feel

buh-resн-net]

**overcooked** zu lange gekocht [tsoo lang-uh gheh-koкнt]

**overexposed** überbelichtet [ōober-buh-lisнt-et]

**overnight** über Nacht [ōober nahкнt]

**oversleep: I overslept** ich habe verschlafen [isн hah-buh fair-shlah-fen]

**overtake** überholen [ōober-hohl-en]

**owe: what do I owe you?** was bin ich Ihnen schuldig? [vass bin isн ee-nen shooldisн]

**own: my own...** mein eigener... [mine i-ghen-er]
**I'm on my own** ich bin allein hier [isн bin al-ine heer]

**owner** der Besitzer [buh-zitser]
*(female)* die Besitzerin

**oxygen** der Sauerstoff [zower-shtoff]

**oysters** Austern [owstern]

# P [pay]

**pack: I haven't packed yet** ich habe noch nicht gepackt [isн hah-buh noкн nisнt gheh-packt]
**can I have a packed lunch?** könnte ich ein Lunchpaket haben? [kurn-tuh isн ine lunch-pakayt hah-ben]

**package tour** die Pauschalreise [pow-shahl-ry-zuh]

**page** *(of book)* die Seite [zy-tuh]
**could you page him?** könnten Sie ihn ausrufen lassen? [kurnten zee een owss-roofen...]

**pain** der Schmerz [shmairts]
**I've got a pain in my...** mir tut mein...weh [meer toot mine...vay]

**pain-killers** die Schmerzmittel [shmairts-mit-el]

**painting** *(picture)* das Gemälde [gheh-mayl-duh]

**Pakistan** Pakistan

**pale** blass [blass]

**pancake** der Pfannkuchen [pfan-kooкнen]

**panties** der Slip
**pants** die Hose [ho-zuh]
   *(underpants)* die Unterhose [oonter-ho-zuh]
**paper** das Papier [pa-peer]
   *(newspaper)* eine Zeitung [tsytoong]
**parcel** ein Paket [pakayt]
**pardon?** *(didn't understand)* wie bitte? [vee bittuh]
   **I beg your pardon** *(sorry)* Entschuldigung [ent-shoold-igoong]
**parents: my parents** meine Eltern
**park** der Park
   **where can I park my car?** wo kann ich parken? [vo...]
   **is it difficult to get parked?** ist es schwierig, einen Parkplatz zu finden? [...shveerish ine-en...]
**Parken nur mit Parkscheibe** parking discs required
**Parken verboten** no parking
**parking ticket** ein Strafzettel [shtrahf-tsettel]
**Parkplatz** car park
**part** ein Teil [tile]
   **a (spare) part** ein Ersatzteil [air-zats-tile]
**partner** *(boyfriend etc)* der Partner
   *(female)* die Partnerin
**party** *(group)* die Gruppe [groop-uh]
   *(celebration)* die Party
   **I'm with the...party** ich bin mit der Gruppe aus...hier [...owss...]
**pass** *(in mountain)* der Pass [pas]
   **he's passed out** er ist ohnmächtig geworden [...ohn-mesh-tish geh-vorden]
**passable** *(road)* passierbar [pas-eer-bar]
**passenger** ein Passagier [pas-aJeer]
   *(woman)* eine Passagierin
**passer-by** ein Passant
   *(woman)* eine Passantin
**passport** der Pass [pas]

✈ You are supposed to carry some form of identification with you at all times, ideally a passport.

**past: in the past** früher [froo-er]
　**it's just past the traffic lights** es kommt gleich nach der Ampel [...glysH nahкн...]
　*go to* **time**
**path** der Weg [vayg]
**patient: be patient** Geduld! [gheh-doolt]
**pattern** das Muster [mooster]
**pavement** der Gehsteig [gay-shtyg]
**pavement café** ein Straßencafé [shtrahssen-kafay]
**pay** bezahlen [buh-tsahlen]
　**can I pay, please** ich möchte gerne zahlen [isH mursHtuh gairn-uh tsahlen]
**peace** *(calm)* die Ruhe [roo-uh]
　*(not war)* der Frieden [freeden]
**peach** ein Pfirsich [pfeer-zisH]
**peanuts** Erdnüsse [airt-nooss-uh]
**pear** eine Birne [beern-uh]
**peas** Erbsen [airp-sen]
**pedal** das Pedal [pay-dahl]
**pedestrian** ein Fußgänger [fooss-genger]
　*(woman)* eine Fußgängerin
**pedestrian crossing** ein Fußgängerüberweg [fooss-genger-oober-vayg]

✈ Be warned: Germans take the red light for pedestrians rather more seriously than we do. On-the-spot fines do happen.

**peg** *(for washing)* eine Wäscheklammer [vesh-uh-]
　*(for tent)* der Hering [hay-ring]
**pen** der Kugelschreiber [kooghel-shryber]
　**have you got a pen?** haben Sie etwas zum Schreiben? [hah-ben zee etvass tsoom shryben]
**pencil** ein Bleistift [bly-shtift]

**penicillin** das Penizillin [pen-its-ileen]
**penknife** das Taschenmesser [tashen-]
**pensioner** der Rentner
　*(woman)* die Rentnerin
**people** die Leute [loytuh]
　**how many people?** wie viele Leute? [vee feel-uh...]
**people carrier** ein Van
**pepper** der Pfeffer
　**a green/red pepper** ein grüner/roter Paprika
　[ine grꝏnuh/ro-tuh...]
**peppermint** das Pfefferminz
**per: per night/week/person** pro Nacht/Woche/
　Person [pro nahкнt/vокн-uh/pair-zohn]
**per cent** Prozent [pro-tsent]
**perfect** perfekt [pair-fekt]
**perfume** das Parfüm [parfꝏm]
**perhaps** vielleicht [fee-lysнt]
**period** *(of time)* der Zeitraum [tsite-rowm]
　*(menstruation)* die Periode [pay-ree-o-duh]
**perm** die Dauerwelle [dow-er-vel-uh]
**permit** eine Genehmigung [gheh-naym-igꝏng]
**person** die Person [pair-zohn]
　**in person** persönlich [pair-zurn-lisн]
**personal stereo** ein Walkman®
**petrol** das Benzin [ben-tseen]
**petrol station** eine Tankstelle [tank-shtel-uh]

　✈ Can be a good place to buy supplies since
　there aren't any 24-hour shops.

**pharmacy** die Apotheke [-taykuh]
　*go to* **chemist**
**phone** das Telefon
　**I'll phone you** ich rufe Sie/dich an *(polite/
　familiar)* [isн roof-uh zee/disн an]
　**I'll phone you back** ich rufe Sie/dich zurück
　*(polite/familiar)* [...tsoo-rꝏck]

**can you phone back in five minutes?** könnten Sie/kannst du in fünf Minuten noch einmal anrufen? *(polite/familiar)* [kurnten zee…minooten noкн ine-mal an-roofen]

---

**can I speak to…?** kann ich…sprechen? […shpresHen]

**could you get the number for me?** könnten Sie die Nummer für mich wählen? [kurnten zee dee noomer foor misH vay-len]

---

*YOU MAY HEAR*
kein Anschluss unter dieser Nummer
*number not in use*
bitte warten *please hold*
leider ist im Moment niemand zu Hause,
bitte hinterlassen Sie eine Nachricht nach
dem Signalton *I'm afraid there's nobody
at home right now, please leave a message
after the tone*

---

**phonebox** die Telefonzelle [tele-fohn-tsel-uh]

✈ You'll probably need a phonecard –
available from post offices or newsagents.

**phonecall** der Anruf [an-roof]
**can I make a phonecall?** kann ich mal telefonieren? […tele-foneer-en]
**phonecard** eine Telefonkarte [tele-fohn-kartuh]
**photograph** die Fotografie [foto-gra-fee]
**would you take a photograph of us/me?** würden Sie ein Bild von uns/mir machen? [voorden zee ine bilt fon oonss/meer mahкнen]
**piano** das Klavier [klaveer]
**pickpocket** ein Taschendieb [tashen-deep]
*(woman)* eine Taschendiebin [tashen-deebin]
**picture** das Bild [bilt]
**pie** *(meat)* die Pastete [pas-tay-tuh]

*(fruit)* der Obstkuchen [ohpst-kooкнen]

**piece: a piece of…** ein Stück… [ine shtŏŏck]

**pig** das Schwein [shvine]

**pigeon** die Taube [towbuh]

**pile-up** die Massenkarambolage [massen-karambo-lah-Juh]

**pill** eine Tablette [tab-let-uh]

**are you on the pill?** nimmst du die Pille? […pil-uh]

**pillow** ein Kissen

**pin** die (Steck)nadel [(shteck)nah-del]

**pineapple** eine Ananas

**pink** rosa

**pint**

> ✈ 1 pint = 0.57 litres

**pipe** die Pfeife [pfyf-uh]

**pity: it's a pity** das ist schade [dass ist shah-duh]

**Pkw, Personenkraftwagen** motor car

**place** der Platz

**is this place taken?** ist hier besetzt? [ist heer buh-zetst]

**do you know any good places to eat?** wissen Sie, wo man gut essen kann? [vissen zee vo man goot…]

**at my place** bei mir (zu Hause) [by meer (tsoo-howz-uh)]

**at your place** bei dir (zu Hause) [by deer…]

**to your place** zu dir [tsoo…]

**plain** einfach [ine-fahкн]

*(food)* gutbürgerlich [goot-bŏŏr-gher-lisн]

*(not patterned)* einfarbig [ine-farbisн]

**plain omelette** einfaches Omelett

**plane** das Flugzeug [floog-tsoyg]

**plant** die Pflanze [pflants-uh]

**plaster** *(cast)* der Gips [ghips]

*(sticking)* das (Heft)pflaster [-pflas-ter]

**plastic** das Plastik
**plastic bag** die Plastiktüte [-tōōt-uh]

✈ Supermarkets charge for plastic bags.

**plate** der Teller
**platform** *(station)* der Bahnsteig [bahn-shtyg]
  **which platform please?** welches Gleis, bitte?
  [velshes glice bittuh]
**play** spielen [shpeelen]
**pleasant** angenehm
**please: could you please...?** könnten Sie,
  bitte,...? [kurnten zee bittuh]
  **(yes) please** ja, bitte [ya...]
**pleasure** das Vergnügen [fair-guh-nōō-ghen]
  **it's a pleasure** gern geschehen [gairn gheh-
  shay-en]
**plenty: plenty of...** eine Menge... [ine-uh meng-
  uh]
  **thank you, that's plenty** danke, das reicht
  [dankuh dass rysHt]
**pliers** die Zange [tsang-uh]
**plug** *(electrical)* der Stecker [shtecker]
  *(for car)* die Zündkerze [tsōōnt-kairts-uh]
  *(for sink)* der Stöpsel [shturp-sel]

✈ Plugs are two-pin in Germany.

**plum** eine Pflaume [pflowm-uh]
**plumber** der Klempner
**plus** plus [plōōss]
**pm: 2 pm** zwei Uhr nachmittags [...nahKH-
  mitahgs]
  **7 pm** sieben Uhr abends [...ah-bents]

✈ The 24-hour clock is commonly used in
  spoken German.

**pocket** die Tasche [tash-uh]
**point: could you point to it?** könnten Sie darauf

*deuten*? [kurnten zee darowf doyten]
**4 point 6** vier Komma sechs
**police** die Polizei [polits-ɪ]
  **get the police** holen Sie die Polizei [ho-len zee dee...]

  ✈ Dial 110.

**policeman** der Polizist [polits-ist]
**police station** die (Polizei)wache [(polits-ɪ-)vahкн-uh]
**policewoman** die Polizistin [polits-istin]
**polish** *(for shoes)* die Schuhcreme [shoo-kraym]
  **can you polish my shoes?** könnten Sie meine Schuhe putzen lassen? [kurnten zee mine-uh shoo-uh pootsen lassen]
**polite** höflich [hurf-lisн]
**polluted** verschmutzt [fair-shmootst]
**pool** *(swimming)* das Schwimmbad [shvim-baht]
**poor: I'm very poor** ich bin sehr arm [isн bin zair...]
  **poor quality** schlechte Qualität [shlesнt-uh kval-itayt]
**pork** das Schweinefleisch [shvine-uh-flysh]
**port** der Hafen [hah-fen]
  *(drink)* der Portwein [-vine]
**porter** *(in hotel)* der Portier [por-tee-ay]
**portrait** das Portrait [por-tray]
**Portugal** Portugal [portoogal]
**posh** vornehm [for-naym]
**possible** möglich [mur-glisн]
  **could you possibly...?** könnten Sie eventuell...? [kurnten zee ay-vent-oo-el]
**post** *(mail)* die Post [posst]
**postbox** der Briefkasten [breefkasten]
**postcard** eine Postkarte [posst-kartuh]
**poste restante** postlagernd [posst-lah-ghernt]
**post office** die Post [posst]

✈ Generally open from 8.00-18.00 Monday to Friday and 8.00-12.00 on Saturdays.

**potatoes** die Kartoffel
**pound** *(weight, money)* das Pfund [pfoont]

✈ pounds/11 x 5 = kilos

| pounds | 1 | 3 | 5 | 6 | 7 | 8 | 9 |
|---|---|---|---|---|---|---|---|
| kilos | 0.4 | 1.4 | 2.3 | 2.7 | 3.2 | 3.6 | 4.1 |

**pour: it's pouring** es gießt [ess geesst]
**power cut** ein Stromausfall [shtrohm-owss-fal]
**power point** eine Steckdose [shteck-dohzuh]
**prawns** Garnelen [garnaylen]
**prefer: I prefer this one** das gefällt mir besser
[...gheh-felt meer...]
   **I'd prefer to...** ich würde lieber... [ish voorduh
   leeber]
   **I'd prefer a...** ich hätte lieber ein... [ish het-uh
   leeber ine]
**pregnant** schwanger [shvanger]
**prescription** das Rezept [rets-ept]
**present: at present** zurzeit [tsoor-tsite]
   **here's a present for you** ein Geschenk für Sie/
   dich *(polite/familiar)* [ine gheh-shenk foor zee/dish]
**president** *(of country)* der Präsident [pray-zident]
   *(woman)* die Präsidentin
**press: could you press these?** könnten Sie die
hier *bügeln*? [kurnten zee dee heer boo-gheln]
**pretty** hübsch [hoopsh]
   **pretty good** ganz gut [gants goot]
   **pretty expensive** ganz schön teuer
   [...shurn...]
**price** der Preis [price]
**priest** der Priester [preester]
   *(woman)* die Priesterin
**prison** das Gefängnis [gheh-fengnis]
**private** privat [pree-vaht]

**probably** wahrscheinlich [var-shine-lisH]
**problem** ein Problem [prob-laym]
  **no problem!** kein Problem! [kine...]
**product** das Produkt [prodookt]
**profit** der Gewinn [gheh-vin]
**promise: do you promise?** versprechen Sie es?
  [fair-shpresHen zee ess]
  *(familiar)* versprichst du es? [fair-shprisHst doo...]
  **I promise** ehrlich! [air-lisH]
**pronounce: how do you pronounce this?** wie
  spricht man das aus? [vee shprisHt man dass owss]
**properly** richtig [risH-tisH]
**prostitute** eine Prostituierte [prostit-oo-eert-uh]
**protect** schützen [shootsen]
**protection factor** der Schutzfaktor [shoots-faktor]
**Protestant** evangelisch [ay-van-gay-lish]
**proud** stolz [shtolts]
**public** die Öffentlichkeit [urfent-lisH-kite]
**public convenience** eine öffentliche Toilette
  [urfent-lisH-uh twalet-uh]

> ✈ Not very many public conveniences in
> Germany; try the railway station; the
> attitude towards using a café etc is the
> same as in Britain.

**public holiday** der gesetzliche Feiertag [gheh-
zets-lisHuh fire-tahg]

> ✈ Public holidays are:
>
> **Neujahr** New Year's Day
> **Karfreitag** Good Friday
> **Ostermontag** Easter Monday
> **Erster Mai** May Day
> **Christi Himmelfahrt** Ascension Day
> **Pfingstmontag** Whit Monday
> **Tag der deutschen Einheit** (3rd October)
> National Unity Day

**(erster) Weihnachtsfeiertag** Christmas Day
**(zweiter) Weihnachtsfeiertag** Boxing Day
There are also a number of regional public holidays, including:
**Dreikönigstag** (Jan 6) Epiphany
**Fronleichnam** Corpus Christi
**Mariä Himmelfahrt** (Aug 15) Assumption
**Reformationstag** (Oct 31) Reformation Day
**Allerheiligen** (Nov 1) All Saints Day
**Buß-und Bettag** (mid Nov) Day of Prayer and Repentance

**pudding** ein Pudding
*(dessert)* der Nachtisch [nahкнtish]
**pull** *(verb)* ziehen [tsee-en]
  **he pulled out in front of me** er ist vor mir ausgeschert [air ist for meer owss-gheh-shayrt]
**pump** die Pumpe [pᴏᴏmp-uh]
**puncture** die Reifenpanne [rife-en-pan-uh]
**pure** rein [rine]
**purple** lila [leela]
**purse** das Portemonnaie [port-mon-ay]
**push** *(verb)* schieben [sheeben]
**pushchair** der Sportwagen [shport-vah-ghen]
**put: where can I put...?** wo kann ich...hintun? [vo kan isн...hintoon]
**pyjamas** ein Schlafanzug [shlahf-an-tsoog]

# Q [koo]

**quality** die Qualität [kval-itayt]
**quarantine** die Quarantäne [kvar-an-tayn-uh]
**quarter** ein Viertel [feertel]
  **a quarter of an hour** eine Viertelstunde [ine-uh...shtᴏᴏnd-uh]
  *go to* **time**

**quay** der Kai [ky]
**question** die Frage [frahg-uh]
**queue** die Schlange [shlang-uh]
**quick** schnell [shnel]
  **that was quick** das ging schnell
**quiet** ruhig [roo-isH]
  **be quiet!** Ruhe! [roo-uh]
**quite** ganz [gants]
  **quite a lot** ganz schön viel [gants shurn feel]

# R [air]

**radiator** *(in car)* der Kühler [kᴕler]
  *(heater)* der Heizkörper [hites-kurper]
**radio** das Radio [rah-dee-o]

> ✈ BFBS (British Forces Radio Station) is useful
> for local travel news and weather forecasts.

**Radweg** cycle path
**rail: by rail** per Bahn [pair...]
**rain** der Regen [ray-ghen]
  **it's raining** es regnet [ess rayg-net]
**raincoat** der Regenmantel [ray-ghen-]
**rally** *(cars)* die Rallye [reli]
**rape** die Vergewaltigung [fair-gheh-val-tigᴕng]
**rare** selten [z-]
  *(steak)* blutig [bloo-tisH]
**raspberry** die Himbeere [him-bair-uh]
**rat** die Ratte [rat-uh]
**Rathaus** town hall
**rather: I'd rather have a...** ich hätte *lieber* ein...
  [isH het-uh leeber ine]
  **I'd rather sit here** ich würde lieber hier sitzen
  [isH vᴕr-duh leeber heer zitsen]
  **I'd rather not** lieber nicht [...nisHt]
  **it's rather hot** es ist ganz schön heiß [ess ist
  gants shurn hice]

**Rauchen verboten** no smoking
**Raucher** smoking compartment
**raw** roh
**razor** ein Rasierapparat [ra-zeer-aparaht]
**read: something to read** etwas zu lesen [etvass tsoo layzen]
**ready: when will it be ready?** wann ist es fertig? [van ist ess fairtisн]
**I'm not ready yet** ich bin noch nicht fertig [isн bin noкн nisнt...]
**real** echt [esнt]
**really** wirklich [veerk-lisн]
**rear-view mirror** der Rückspiegel [rооck-shpee-ghel]
**reasonable** vernünftig [fair-nооnf-tisн]
**receipt** die Quittung [kvitoong]
**can I have a receipt please?** kann ich bitte eine Quittung haben? [kan isн bittuh ine-uh... hah-ben]
**recently** kürzlich [kооrts-lisн]
**reception** der Empfang
**in reception** am Empfang
**receptionist** der Empfangschef
*(woman)* die Empfangsdame [-dah-muh]
**rechts fahren** keep right
**recipe** das Rezept [rets-ept]
**recommend: can you recommend...?** können Sie...empfehlen? [kurnen zee...emp-fay-len]
**red** rot [roht]
**reduction** *(in price)* die Ermäßigung [air-mace-igoong]
**red wine** ein Rotwein [roht-vine]
**refuse: I refuse** ich weigere mich [isн vy-guh-ruh misн]
**region** das Gebiet [gheh-beet]
**registered: I want to send this registered** ich möchte das *per Einschreiben* schicken [isн

mursHtuh das pair ine-shry-ben shicken]

**relax: I just want to relax** ich will mich nur
*entspannen* [isH vil misH noor ent-shpan-en]

**relax!** immer mit der Ruhe! [...dair roo-uh]

**remember: don't you remember?** erinnern Sie
sich nicht mehr? [air-inern zee zisH nisHt mair]
*(familiar)* errinerst du dich nicht mehr?

**I don't remember** ich erinnere mich nicht [isH
air-iner-ruh misH nisHt]

**rent: can I rent a car/bicycle?** kann ich ein
Auto/Fahrrad *mieten?* [...meeten]

---

*YOU MAY HEAR*
welche Marke? *what type?*
für wie viele Tage? *for how many days?*
bringen Sie es bis...zurück *bring it back
before...*
ohne Kilometerbeschränkung *unlimited
mileage*

---

**rental car** der Mietwagen [meet-vah-ghen]

**rep** der Vertreter [fair-tray-ter]
*(woman)* die Vertreterin
*(activities organizer)* der Animateur [animatur]
*(woman)* die Animateurin

**repair: can you repair it?** können Sie es
reparieren? [kurnen zee ess rep-a-ree-ren]

**repeat: could you repeat that?** könnten Sie das
*wiederholen?* [kurnten zee dass veeder-hohl-en]

**reputation** der Ruf [roof]

**rescue** *(verb)* retten

**reservation** die Reservierung [rez-air-veeroong]

**I want to make a reservation for...** *(in
restaurant)* ich möchte einen Tisch für...bestellen
[isH mursHtuh ine-en tisH fŏŏr...buh-shtellen]

**reserve: can I reserve a seat?** kann ich einen
Platz reservieren? [kan isH ine-en plats rez-air-
vee-ren]

> *YOU MAY THEN HEAR*
> für welche Uhrzeit? *for what time?*
> auf welchen Namen? *in what name?*

**responsible** verantwortlich [fair-ant-vort-lisн]

**rest: I've come here for a rest** ich bin hier, um mal auszuspannen [isн bin heer oom mal owss-stoo-shpan-en]

  **you keep the rest** der Rest ist für Sie [...ist foor zee]

**restaurant** ein Restaurant [restorong]

**restaurant car** der Speisewagen [shpy-zuh-vah-ghen]

**retired** pensioniert [pen-zee-o-neert]

**return: a return to...** eine Rückfahrkarte nach... [roock-far-kartuh nahкн]

**reverse charge call** ein R-Gespräch [air-gheh-shpraysн]

**reverse gear** der Rückwärtsgang [roock-vairts-]

**rheumatism** das Rheuma [roy-ma]

**rib** eine Rippe [rip-uh]

**rice** der Reis [rice]

**rich** *(person)* reich [rysн]

**ridiculous** lächerlich [lesн-er-lisн]

**right: that's right** das stimmt [dass shtimt]

  **you're right** Sie haben Recht [zee hah-ben resнt]

  **on the right** rechts [resнts]

  **right!** *(understood)* gut! [goot]

**righthand drive** rechts gesteuert [resнts gheh-shtoy-ert]

**ring** *(on finger)* der Ring

**ripe** reif [rife]

**rip-off: it's a rip-off** das ist Wucher! [dass ist vooкнer]

**river** der Fluss [flooss]

**road** die Straße [shtrahss-uh]

**which is the road to...?** wo geht es nach...?
[vo gayt ess nahKH]

**road map** eine Straßenkarte [shtrah-sen-kartuh]

**rob: I've been robbed** ich bin *bestohlen* worden
[iSH bin buh-shtohl-en vorden]

**rock** der Fels [felss]

**whisky on the rocks** Whisky mit Eis [...ice]

**roll** *(bread)* ein Brötchen [brurt-SHen]

**romantic** romantisch [-tish]

**roof** das Dach [dahKH]

**roof box** der Dachkoffer [dahKH-]

**roof rack** der Gepäckträger [gheh-peck-tray-gher]

**room** das Zimmer [tsimmer]

**have you got a single room?** haben Sie ein
Einzelzimmer? [hah-ben zee ine ine-tsel-]

**have you got a double room?** haben Sie ein
Doppelzimmer?

---

**for one night** für eine Nacht [foor ine-uh nahKHt]

**for three nights** für drei Nächte [...dry neshtuh]

---

*YOU MAY THEN HEAR*
tut mir Leid *sorry*
wir sind voll ausgebucht *we're full*
wir haben nichts mehr frei *there are no rooms left*
mit Bad oder ohne? *with or without bath?*
Übernachtung mit Frühstück *bed and breakfast*

---

**room service** der Zimmerservice [tsimmer-serviss]

**rope** das Seil [zile]

**rose** die Rose [ro-zuh]

**rough** *(sea)* stürmisch [shtoormish]

**roughly** *(approx)* ungefähr [oon-gheh-fair]

**round** *(circular)* rund [roont]

   **it's my round** das ist meine Runde [...mine-uh roond-uh]

**roundabout** *(on road)* der Kreisverkehr [krice-fair-kair]

   ✈ Drivers on the roundabout have priority. Remember that they will be coming from the left.

**route** die Strecke [shtreck-uh]

   **which is the prettiest/fastest route?** was ist die schönste/schnellste Strecke? [...shurn-stuh/ shnel-stuh...]

**rowing boat** das Ruderboot [rooder-boht]

**rubber** der Gummi [goomee]

**rubber band** das Gummiband [goomee-bant]

**rubbish** *(waste)* der Abfall [ap-fal]

   *(poor quality goods)* der Mist

   **rubbish!** Quatsch! [kvatsh]

   ✈ You'll find different bins for different types of rubbish. Germany is a very eco-friendly country.

**rucksack** der Rucksack [roock-zack]

**rude** unhöflich [oon-hurf-lisH]

**Ruhetag** closed all day

**ruin** die Ruine [roo-een-uh]

**rum** ein Rum [room]

   **a rum and coke** eine Cola mit Rum

**run: hurry, run!** beeil dich, *lauf!* [buh-ile disH lowf]

   **I've run out of petrol/money** mir ist das Benzin/Geld ausgegangen [meer ist dass bentseen/ghelt owss-gheh-gang-en]

# S [ess]

**sad** traurig [trow-risH]

**safe** sicher [zisHer]
  **will it be safe here?** ist es hier sicher? [ist ess heer…]
  **is it safe to swim here?** kann man hier ohne Gefahr schwimmen? […o-nuh geh-fahr shvimmen]

**safety** die Sicherheit [zisHer-hite]

**safety pin** eine Sicherheitsnadel [zisHer-hites-nah-del]

**sail: can we go sailing?** können wir segeln gehen? [kurnen veer zay-gheln gay-en]

**sailboard** ein Surfbrett

**sailor** ein Seemann [zay-man]
  *(sport)* der Segler [zaygler]
  *(woman)* die Seglerin

**salad** ein Salat [zal-aht]

**salami** die Salami [z-]

**sale: is it for sale?** kann man das kaufen? […kow-fen]

**salmon** der Lachs [laks]

**salt** das Salz [zalts]

**same: the same** derselbe/dieselbe/dasselbe [dair-/dee-/dass-zelbuh]
  **the same again, please** das gleiche nochmal [dass glysH-uh noкHmal bittuh]
  **it's all the same to me** es ist mir egal [ess ist meer ay-gahl]

**sand** der Sand [zant]

**sandals** die Sandalen [zan-dahlen]

**sandwich** ein Sandwich
  **a ham/cheese sandwich** ein Schinken-/Käsesandwich [shinken/kay-zuh-]

✈ In a Gasthaus you could also ask for a
**Schinkenbrot** or **Käsebrot** which will be
more like an open sandwich.

**sanitary towels** die Damenbinden [dah-men-bin-
den]
**satisfactory** befriedigend [buh-freed-ighent]
**Saturday** Samstag [zamz-tahg]
**sauce** die Soße [zo-suh]
**saucepan** der Kochtopf [koкн-topf]
**saucer** der Unterteller [oonter-]
**sauna** eine Sauna [zow-na]
**sausage** eine Wurst [voorst]

✈ Main types are **Bratwurst** [braht-] (fried),
**Bockwurst** (boiled) and **Currywurst**.
Usually served with a roll and optional
mustard (**Senf**).

**say** sagen [zah-ghen]
 **how do you say...in German?** was heißt...auf
deutsch? [vass hysst...owf doytsh]
 **what did he say?** was hat er gesagt? [vass hat
air gheh-zahgt]
**S-Bahn** suburban railway
**scarf** der Schal [shahl]
 *(for head)* das Kopftuch [-tooкн]
 *(for neck)* das Halstuch [halss-tooкн]
**scenery** die Landschaft [lant-shafft]
**schedule** der Zeitplan [tsite-plahn]
 *(programme)* das Programm
 **on schedule** pünktlich [pöonkt-lisн]
 **behind schedule** verspätet [fair-shpaytet]
**scheduled flight** der Linienflug [leen-ee-en-
floog]
**Schlafwagen** sleeper
**Schleuderpreise** prices slashed
**Schließfächer** luggage lockers

**Schlussverkauf** sale
**schnaps** ein Schnaps

> ✈ Try North German **Korn** (grain), Black
> Forest **Kirsch** (cherries) or **Steinhäger**
> [shtine-hay-gher] (juniper berries).

**school** die Schule [shool-uh]
**Schwimmbad** swimming pool
**scissors: a pair of scissors** eine Schere [ine-uh
shay-ruh]
**scooter** der (Motor)roller [mo-tor-rol-er]
**Scotland** Schottland [shot-lant]
**Scottish** schottisch [shotish]
**scream** *(verb)* schreien [shry-en]
*(noun)* der Schrei [shry]
**screw** die Schraube [shrow-buh]
**screwdriver** der Schraubenzieher [shrow-ben-
tsee-er]
**sea** das Meer [mayr]
**by the sea** am Meer
**seafood** Meeresfrüchte [mayr-ess-frōōsht-uh]
**search** *(verb)* suchen [zooKH-en]
**search party** eine Suchmannschaft [zooKH-man-
shafft]
**seasick: I get seasick** ich werde seekrank [iSH
vairduh zay-]
**seaside: let's go to the seaside** fahren wir ans
Meer
**season** die Saison [sez-ong]
**in the high season** in der Hochsaison [in dair
hohKH-]
**in the low season** in der Nebensaison [...nay-
ben-]
**seasoning** das Gewürz [gheh-vōōrts]
**seat** der (Sitz)platz
**is this somebody's seat?** sitzt hier jemand?
[zitst heer yay-mant]

**seat belt** der Sicherheitsgurt [ziSHer-hites-goort]
**second** *(adjective)* zweite [tsvyt-uh]
  *(of time)* die Sekunde [zekoonduh]
**secondhand** gebraucht [geh-browKHt]
**see** sehen [zay-en]
  **have you seen...?** haben Sie...gesehen? [hah-ben zee...gheh-zay-en]
  **can I see the room?** kann ich mir das Zimmer anschauen? [kan iSH meer dass tsimmer an-show-en]
  **see you!** tschüs [tshooss]
  **see you tonight** bis heute Abend [...hoytuh ahbent]
  **oh, I see** ach so! [ahKH zo]
**self-catering apartment** ein Apartment für Selbstversorger [...foor zelpst-fair-zorger]
**self-service** Selbstbedienung [zelpst-buh-deen-oong]
**sell** verkaufen [fair-kowfen]
**send** schicken [shicken]
  **I want to send this to England** ich möchte das nach England schicken [iSH murSHtuh dass nahKH...]
**sensitive** empfindlich [emp-fint-liSH]
**separate** *(adjective)* getrennt
  **I'm separated** wir leben getrennt [veer lay-ben...]
**separately: can we pay separately?** können wir getrennt zahlen? [kurnen veer...tsah-len]
**September** September [z-]
**serious** ernst [airnst]
  **I'm serious** ich meine das ernst [iSH mine-uh dass...]
  **this is serious** das ist ernst
  **is it serious, doctor?** ist es schlimm? [ist ess shlim]
**service: is service included?** ist der Service

eingeschlossen? [...ine-geh-shlossen]

**service station** eine Tankstelle [tank-shtel-uh]

**services** *(on motorway)* eine Raststätte [rast-shtet-uh]

**serviette** eine Serviette [zair-vee-et-uh]

**several** mehrere [mair-uh-ruh]

**sex** Sex

**sexy** sexy

**shade: in the shade** im Schatten [...shat-en]

**shake** schütteln [shoot-eln]

**to shake hands** die Hand schütteln [dee hant...]

> ✈ It's normal to shake hands each time
> you meet someone and when you leave
> someone.

**shallow** seicht [zysHt]

**shame: what a shame!** wie schade! [vee shah-duh]

**shampoo** das Shampoo

**shandy** ein Bier mit Limonade [beer mit lee-mo-nah-duh]

> ✈ In South Germany ask for **einen Radler**; in
> the north it's called **ein Alsterwasser**. Or
> you could try **ein Altbier-Cola** (dark beer
> with coke).

**share** *(room, table)* teilen [tile-en]

**sharp** scharf [sharf]

*(taste)* herb [hairp]

*(pain)* heftig

**shave** rasieren [razee-ren]

**shaver** der Rasierapparat [razeer-aparaht]

**shaving foam** der Rasierschaum [razeer-showm]

**shaving point** eine Steckdose für Rasierapparate [shteck-dohzuh foor...]

**she** sie [zee]

**sheet** das Leintuch [line-tookH]

**shelf** das Regal [ray-gahl]

**shell** *(sea-)* eine Muschel [mooshel]

**shellfish** Meeresfrüchte [mayr-ess-frooSH-tuh]

**shelter** der Unterstand [oonter-shtant]

  **can we shelter here?** können wir hier unterstehen? [kurnen veer heer oonter-shtay-en]

**sherry** ein Sherry

**ship** das Schiff [shif]

**shirt** das Hemd [hemt]

**shit!** Scheiße! [shy-suh]

**shock** der Schock

  **I got an electric shock from the...** ich habe von dem...einen Schlag bekommen [isH hah-buh fon daym...ine-en shlahg buh-]

**shock-absorber** der Stoßdämpfer [shtohss-dempfer]

**shoelaces** Schnürsenkel [shnoor-zenkel]

**shoes** die Schuhe [shoo-uh]

| ✈ men: | | | | | | | 40 | 41 | 42 | 43 | 44 | 45 |
|---|---|---|---|---|---|---|---|---|---|---|---|---|
| women: | 36 | 37 | 38 | 39 | 40 | 41 | | | | | | |
| UK: | 3 | 4 | 5 | 6 | 7 | 8 | 9 | 10 | 11 | | | |

**shop** das Geschäft [gheh-sheft]

  **I've some shopping to do** ich muss noch ein paar Einkäufe erledigen [isH mooss nokH ine par ine-koy-fuh air-lay-dig-en]

  ✈ Generally open from 9.30 am-8.00 pm Mon-Fri. On Saturdays closing hours are 8.00 pm in the cities, 6.00 pm in towns and 1.00 pm in small towns and villages. On Sundays all shops are closed. There are no 24-hour shops. But bigger petrol stations open day and night and sell basics like milk, bread, ready meals or toiletries.

**shop assistant** der Verkäufer [fair-koyfer] *(woman)* die Verkäuferin

**short** kurz [koorts]
  *(person)* klein [kline]
**short cut** eine Abkürzung [ap-koorts-oong]
**shorts** die Shorts
**shoulder** die Schulter [shoolter]
**shout** rufen [roofen]
**show: please show me** bitte zeigen Sie es mir
  [bittuh tsy-ghen zee ess meer]
**shower: with shower** mit Dusche [...doosh-uh]
**shrimps** Garnelen [gar-nay-len]
**shut** schließen [shlee-sen]
  **they're shut** es ist zu [...tsoo]
  **when do you shut?** wann machen Sie zu? [van
  maHKHen zee tsoo]
  **shut up!** halt den Mund! [hallt dayn moont]
**shy** schüchtern [shooSH-tern]
**sick** krank
  **I feel sick** mir ist schlecht [meer ist shlesHt]
  **he's been sick** er hat gebrochen [air hat geh-
  broKH-en]
**side** die Seite [zy-tuh]
  **by the side of the road** an der Straße [...
  shtrahss-uh]
**side street** eine Nebenstraße [nay-ben-shtrahss-uh]
**sight: the sights of...** die Sehenswürdigkeiten
  von... [dee zay-enz-voord-isH-kite-en fon]
**sightseeing tour** eine Rundreise [roont-ry-zuh]
  *(of town)* eine Stadtrundfahrt [shtat-roont-fart]
**sign** *(notice)* das Schild [shilt]
**signal: he didn't signal** er hat kein Zeichen
  gegeben [air hat kine tsysHen gheh-gay-ben]
**signature** die Unterschrift [oonter-shrift]
**silence** die Stille [shtil-uh]
**silencer** die Schalldämpfer [shal-dem-pfer]
**silk** die Seide [zy-duh]
**silly** dumm [doomm]
**silver** das Silber [zilber]

**similar** ähnlich [ayn-lisH]

**simple** einfach [ine-fahкн]

**since: since last week** seit letzter Woche [zite lets-ter voкн-uh]

   **since we arrived** seit wir da sind

   *(because)* weil [vile]

**sincere** aufrichtig [owf-risн-tisн]

**sing** singen [zingen]

**single: I'm single** ich bin ledig [isн bin lay-disн]

   *(no partner)* ich bin 'Single'

   **a single to...** einmal einfach nach... [ine-mal ine-fahкн nahкн]

**single room** ein Einzelzimmer [ine-tsel-tsimmer]

**sister: my sister** meine Schwester [mine-uh shvester]

**sit: can I sit here?** kann ich mich hierher setzen? [kan isн misн heer-hair zetsen]

**size** die Größe [grur-suh]

**skates** die Schlittschuhe [shlit-shoo-uh]

**ski** der Ski [shee]

   *(verb)* Ski fahren [shee...]

**ski boots** die Skistiefel [shee-shteefel]

**skid** schleudern [shloy-dern]

**skiing** das Skifahren [shee-]

**ski lift** der Skilift [shee-]

**skin** die Haut [howt]

**ski pants** die Skihose [shee-ho-zuh]

**ski pole** der Skistock [shee-shtock]

**skirt** der Rock

**ski slope** die Piste [piss-tuh]

**ski wax** das Skiwachs [shee-vaks]

**sky** der Himmel

**sledge** der Schlitten [sh-]

**sleep: I can't sleep** ich kann nicht schlafen [isн kan nisнt shlah-fen]

**sleeper** *(rail)* der Schlafwagen [shlahf-vah-ghen]

**sleeping bag** der Schlafsack [shlahf-zack]

**sleeping pill** eine Schlaftablette [shlahf-tab-letuh]
**sleeve** der Ärmel [air-mel]
**slide** *(photo)* das Dia [dee-a]
**slow** langsam [lang-zahm]
  **could you speak a little slower?** könnten Sie etwas langsamer sprechen? [kurnten zee etvass lang-zahmer shpresнen]
**slowly** langsam [lang-zahm]
**small** klein [kline]
  **smaller notes** kleinere Geldscheine [kline-eruh ghelt-shine-uh]
**small change** das Kleingeld [kline-ghelt]
**smell: there's a funny smell** hier riecht es komisch [heer reesнt ess ko-misн]
  **it smells** es stinkt [ess shtinkt]
**smile** *(verb)* lächeln [lesн-eln]
**smoke** der Rauch [rowкн]
  **do you smoke?** rauchen Sie? [rowкнen zee]
  **can I smoke?** darf ich rauchen?
**snack: can we just have a snack?** könnten wir einen *Imbiss* bekommen? [kurnen veer ine-en im-biss buh-kommen]

➤ Look for an **Imbissstube** or **Schnellimbiss**; they sell sausages, chips or kebabs. They're often on the street and with no seats.

**snow** der Schnee [shnay]
  **it's snowing** es schneit [ess shnite]
**snow chains** die Schneeketten [shnay-ket-en]

➤ Can be hired from ADAC depots.

**so: it's so hot** es ist so warm
  **not so much** nicht so viel [nisнt zo feel]
  **so am/do I** ich auch [isн owкн]
**soap** die Seife [zyfuh]
**soap powder** das Seifenpulver [zy-fen-pɵolver]
**sober** nüchtern [nᴏᴏsнtern]

**socks** die Socken [zock-en]

**soda (water)** das Soda(wasser) [-vasser]

**soft drink** ein alkoholfreies Getränk [al-ko-hohl-fry-ess gheh-trenk]

Sofortreinigung fast-service dry cleaner's

**sole** die Sohle [zo-luh]

**some: some people** einige Leute [ine-ig-uh loytuh]

**can I have some grapes/some bread?** kann ich *ein paar* Trauben/*etwas* Brot haben? [...ine par trow-ben/etvass broht...]

**somebody** jemand [yay-mant]

**something** etwas [etvass]

**sometimes** manchmal [mansH-mal]

**somewhere** irgendwo [eer-ghent-vo]

**son: my son** mein Sohn [mine zohn]

Sonderangebot special offer

**song** das Lied [leet]

**soon** bald [balt]

**as soon as possible** so bald wie möglich [zo... vee mur-glisH]

**sooner** früher [frꝏ-er]

**sore: it's sore** es tut weh [ess toot vay]

**sore throat** das Halsweh [halss-vay]

**sorry: (I'm) sorry** Entschuldigung! [ent-shool-digꝏng]

**sorry?** wie bitte? [vee bittuh]

**sort: this sort** diese Art [deez-uh...]

**what sort of...?** was für ein..? [vass fꝏr ine]

**will you sort it out?** können Sie das in Ordnung bringen? [kurnen zee dass in ordnꝏng...]

**so-so** so la la

**soup** die Suppe [zꝏp-uh]

**sour** sauer [zow-er]

**south** der Süden [zꝏ-den]

**South Africa** Südafrika [zꝏd-afrika]

**souvenir** ein Souvenir
**spade** ein Spaten [shpaht-en]
   *(child's)* eine Schaufel [show-fel]
**Spain** Spanien [shpahnee-en]
**spanner** ein Schraubenschlüssel [shrow-ben-shlōōssel]
**spare part** das Ersatzteil [air-zats-tile]
**spare wheel** das Ersatzrad [air-zats-raht]
**Sparkasse** savings bank
**spark plug** eine Zündkerze [tsōōnt-kairts-uh]
**speak** sprechen [shpreSHen]
   **do you speak English?** sprechen Sie Englisch? […zee eng-lish]
   **I don't speak German** ich kann kein Deutsch [ish kan kine doytsh]
**special** besonderer [buh-zon-der-ruh]
**specialist** der Fachmann [faHKH-man]
   *(woman)* die Fachfrau [-frow]
**spectacles** die Brille [bril-uh]
**speed** die Geschwindigkeit [geh-shvin-dish-kite]
   **he was speeding** er ist zu schnell gefahren [air ist tsoo shnel geh-faren]
**speed limit** die Geschwindigkeitsbegrenzung [geh-shvin-dish-kites-buh-grents-ōong]

   ✈ Speed limits are 50 kph (31 mph) in town; 100 kph (62 mph) out of town; motorways are derestricted for cars unless there is a speed limit sign (and there are quite a few) and for lorries and caravans it's 100 kph (62 mph).

**speedometer** der Tachometer [taKH-o-may-ter]
**Speisewagen** dining car
**spend** *(money)* ausgeben [owss-gay-ben]
**spice** das Gewürz [geh-vōorts]
   **is it spicy?** ist es stark gewürzt? […shtark geh-vōortst]

**spider** eine Spinne [shpin-uh]
**spoon** der Löffel [lur-fel]
**Sprechstunde** surgery hours
**sprain: I've sprained my...** ich habe mir den/
das...verstaucht [ish hah-buh meer dayn/dass...
fair-shtowkht]
**spring** *(of car, seat)* die Feder [fay-der]
*(season)* der Frühling [frōō-ling]
**square** *(in town)* der Platz
  **two square metres** zwei Quadratmeter
  [tsvy kvad-raht-may-ter]
**Stadtmitte** city centre; town centre
**stairs** die Treppe [trep-uh]
**stalls** das Parkett
**stamp** eine Briefmarke [breef-mark-uh]
  **two stamps for England** zwei Briefmarken
  nach England [tsvy...nahkh eng-lant]
**stand** *(at fair)* der Stand [shtant]
**stand-by: to fly stand-by** Stand-by fliegen
  [...fleeghen]
**star** der Stern [shtairn]
**start: when does it start?** wann fängt es an?
  [van fengt ess an]
  **my car won't start** mein Auto springt nicht an
  [mine owto shpringt nisht an]
**starter** *(of car)* der Anlasser
  *(food)* das 'Hors d'œuvre'
**starving: I'm starving** ich habe einen
  Riesenhunger [ish hah-buh ine-en ree-zen-hoong-
  er]
**station** der Bahnhof [bahn-hohff]
**statue** die Statue [shtaht-oo-uh]
**stay** der Aufenthalt [owf-enthallt]
  **we enjoyed our stay** es hat uns hier gut
  gefallen [ess hat oonss heer goot gheh-fal-en]
  **stay there** bleiben Sie dort! [bly-ben zee...]
  **I'm staying at...** ich wohne im... [ish vo-nuh...]

**steak** ein 'Steak'

> *YOU MAY HEAR*
> wie möchten Sie Ihr Steak gebraten
> haben? *how would you like your steak?*
> ganz durch? *well done?*
> halb durch? *medium?*
> blutig? *rare?*

**steal: my wallet's been stolen** man hat mir
meine Brieftasche gestohlen [man hat meer
m<small>i</small>ne-uh br<small>ee</small>f-tash-uh gheh-sht<small>oh</small>l-en]
**steep** steil [shtile]
**steering** die Lenkung [l<small>e</small>nk<small>oo</small>ng]
**steering wheel** das Steuerrad [sht<small>oy</small>-er-raht]
**Stehplätze** standing room
**step** *(of stairs)* die Stufe [sht<small>oo</small>f-uh]
**sterling** Sterling
**stewardess** die Stewardess
**sticking plaster** das Heftpflaster [h<small>e</small>ft-pflass-ter]
**sticky** klebrig [kl<small>ay</small>-bri<small>SH</small>]
**stiff** steif [shtife]
**still: keep still** halten Sie still [h<small>a</small>l-ten zee shtil]
*(familiar)* halt still
  **I'm still here** ich bin immer noch da [...<small>NOKH</small>...]
  **I'm still waiting** ich warte noch immer [...vart-
  uh...]
**sting: I've been stung** ich bin gestochen worden
[i<small>SH</small> bin gheh-sht<small>oKH</small>en v<small>o</small>rden]
**stink** der Gestank [gheh-sht<small>a</small>nk]
**stink: it stinks** es stinkt [...shtinkt]
**Stock(werk)** floor, storey
**stomach** der Magen [m<small>a</small>h-ghen]
  **have you got something for an upset
  stomach?** haben Sie etwas gegen
  Magenbeschwerden? [h<small>a</small>h-ben zee etvass g<small>ay</small>-
  ghen m<small>a</small>h-ghen-buh-shvairden]
**stomach-ache: I have a stomach-ache** ich

habe Magenschmerzen [isH hah-buh mah-ghen-shmairtsen]

**stone** der Stein [shtine]

✈ 1 stone = 6.35 kilos

**stop** *(for buses)* die Haltestelle [halltuh-shtel-uh]
  **stop!** halt! [hallt]
  **do you stop near...?** halten Sie in der Nähe von...? [hallten zee in dair nay-uh fon]
  **could you stop here?** könnten Sie hier anhalten? [kurnten zee heer an-hallten]
**stop-over** eine Zwischenstation [tsvishen-shtats-yohn]
  *(flying)* eine Zwischenlandung
**storm** der Sturm [shtoorm]
**strafbar: ...ist strafbar** ...is a punishable offence
**straight** gerade [gheh-rah-duh]
  **go straight on** gehen Sie geradeaus [gay-en zee gheh-rah-duh-owss]
  **a straight whisky** ein Whisky pur [...poor]
**straightaway** sofort [zo-fort]
**strange** *(odd)* seltsam [zelt-zahm]
  *(unknown)* fremd [fremt]
**stranger** der Fremde [fremd-uh]
  *(woman)* die Fremde
  **I'm a stranger here** ich bin fremd hier [isH bin fremt heer]
**strawberry** eine Erdbeere [airt-bair-uh]
**street** die Straße [shtrahss-uh]
**street map** ein Stadtplan [shtat-plahn]
**strengstens untersagt** strictly forbidden
**string: have you got any string?** haben Sie eine Schnur? [hah-ben zee ine-uh shnoor]
**stroke: he's had a stroke** er hat einen Schlaganfall bekommen [air hat ine-en shlahg-an-fal buh-kommen]
**strong** stark [shtark]

**stuck: the drawer's stuck** die Schublade klemmt [shoop-lah-duh…]

**student** der Student [shtoo-dent]
 *(female)* die Studentin

**stupid** dumm [doom]

**such: such a lot** so viel [zo feel]

**suddenly** plötzlich [plurts-lisH]

**sugar** der Zucker [tsoocker]

**suit** *(man's)* der Anzug [an-tsoog]
 *(woman's)* das Kostüm [kostoom]

**suitable** passend [pa-sent]

**suitcase** der Koffer

**summer** der Sommer [zommer]

**sun** die Sonne [zonn-uh]
 **in the sun** in der Sonne
 **out of the sun** im Schatten [im shat-en]

**sunbathe** sonnenbaden [zonnen-bah-den]

**sun block** eine Sonnenschutzcreme [zonnen-shoots-kraym]

**sunburn** der Sonnenbrand [zonnen-brant]

**sun cream** eine Sonnencreme [zonnen-kraym]

**Sunday** Sonntag [zonn-tahg]

**sunglasses** die Sonnenbrille [zonnen-bril-uh]

**sun lounger** eine Liege [leeg-uh]

**sunstroke** der Sonnenstich [zonnen-shtisH]

**suntan** die Bräune [broy-nuh]

**suntan oil** das Sonnenöl [zonnen-url]

**supermarket** der Supermarkt [zooper-]

**supper** das Abendessen [ah-bent-]

**sure: I'm not sure** ich bin nicht sicher [isH bin nisHt zisHer]
 **are you sure?** sind Sie sicher? [zint zee…]
 **sure!** sicher!

**surname** der Nachname [nahкн-nah-muh]

**Süßwaren** confectionery

**swearword** der Fluch [flooкн]

**sweat** *(verb)* schwitzen [shvitsen]

**sweater** der Pullover
**sweet** *(dessert)* der Nachtisch [nahKH-tish]
  **it's too sweet** es ist zu süß [...zōōss]
**sweets** die Süßigkeiten [zōōss-isH-kite-en]
**swerve: I had to swerve** ich musste
  ausschwenken [isH mōōss-tuh owss-shvenken]
**swim: I'm going for a swim** ich gehe
  schwimmen [isH gay-uh shvimmen]
  **I can't swim** ich kann nicht schwimmen
  **let's go for a swim** gehen wir schwimmen
**swimming costume** der Badeanzug [bah-duh-
  an-tsoog]
**swimming pool** das Schwimmbad [shvim-baht]
**Swiss** schweizerisch [shvites-erish]
  *(man)* der Schweizer [shvites-er]
  *(woman)* die Schweizerin
**switch** der Schalter [shalter]
  **to switch on** anschalten [an-shalten]
  **to switch off** abschalten [ap-shalten]
**Switzerland** die Schweiz [shvites]
  **in Switzerland** in der Schweiz

# T [tay]

**table** ein Tisch [tish]
  **a table for four** ein Tisch für vier [ine...fōōr...]
**table wine** Tafelwein [tah-fel-vine]
**take** nehmen [nay-men]
  **can I take this?** kann ich das mitnehmen?
  **will you take me to the airport?** bringen Sie
  mich zum Flughafen? [...zee misH tsoom floog-
  hah-fen]
  **how long will it take?** wie lange dauert es?
  [vee lang-uh dowert ess]
  **somebody has taken my bags** jemand hat
  mein Gepäck mitgenommen [yay-mant hat mine
  gheh-peck mit-gheh-nommen]

**can I take you out tonight?** kann ich Sie/dich
für heute Abend einladen? *(polite/familiar)* [kan
isH zee/disH fŏŏr hoytuh ah-bent ine-lah-den]
  **is this seat taken?** sitzt hier jemand? [zitst heer
yay-mant]
  **I'll take it** ich nehme es [isH nay-muh ess]
**talk** *(verb)* sprechen [shpresHen]
**tall** *(person)* groß [grohss]
  *(building)* hoch [hohkH]
**tampons** die Tampons
**tan** die Bräune [broy-nuh]
**tank** *(of car)* der Tank
**Tankstelle** petrol station
**tap** der Hahn
**tape** *(cassette)* das Tonband [tohn-bant]
**tape-recorder** das Tonbandgerät [tohn-bant-
gheh-rayt]
**tariff** der Tarif [tah-reef]
**taste** der Geschmack [gheh-shmack]
  **can I taste it?** kann ich es versuchen? [kan isH
ess fair-zookHen]
**taxi** ein Taxi
  **will you get me a taxi?** rufen Sie mir bitte ein
Taxi! [roofen zee meer bittuh...]
  **where can I get a taxi?** wo bekomme ich ein
Taxi? [vo buh-kommuh isH...]

✈ Not so common to hail a taxi on the
  street.

**taxi-driver** der Taxifahrer
  *(woman)* die Taxifahrerin
**tea** der Tee [tay]
  **could I have a cup of tea?** könnte ich eine
Tasse Tee haben? [kurntuh isH ine-uh tass-uh tay
hah-ben]
  **could I have a pot of tea?** könnte ich ein
Kännchen Tee haben? [...ine ken-sHen...]

> *YOU MAY THEN HEAR*
> mit Milch? *with milk***?**
> mit Zitrone? *with lemon***?**

**teach: could you teach me some German?**
könnten Sie mir ein paar Worte Deutsch
beibringen? [kurnten zee meer ine par vort-uh
doytsh by-bringen]
**teacher** der Lehrer [lair-uh]
*(woman)* die Lehrerin
**telephone** das Telefon
*go to* **phone**
**telephone directory** das Telefonbuch [-booкн]
**television** das Fernsehen [fairn-zay-en]
**I'd like to watch television** ich möchte gerne
fernsehen [isн mursнtuh gairn-uh...]
**tell: could you tell me where...?** könnten Sie
mir sagen, wo...? [kurnten zee meer zahgen vo]
**could you tell him...?** könnten Sie ihm
sagen...? [...eem...]
**I told him that...** ich habe ihm gesagt, dass...
[...hah-buh eem gheh-zahgt...]
**temperature** *(weather etc)* die Temperatur [-toor]
**he's got a temperature** er hat Fieber [air hat
feeber]
**tennis** Tennis
**tennis ball** der Tennisball [-bal]
**tennis court** der Tennisplatz
**tennis racket** der Tennisschläger [-shlay-gher]
**tent** das Zelt [tselt]
**terminus** die Endstation [ent-shtats-yohn]
**terrible** schrecklich [shreck-lisн]
**terrific** sagenhaft [zah-ghen-haft]
**text: I'll text you** ich schicke dir eine *SMS* [isн
shick-uh deer ine-uh ess-em-ess]
**text message** eine SMS [ess-em-ess]
**than** als [alss]

**bigger than...** größer als... [grurser...]
**thanks, thank you** danke (schön) [dank-uh (shurn)]

  **thank you very much** vielen Dank [feelen...]
  **no thank you** nein danke [nine...]
  **thank you for your help** vielen Dank für Ihre Hilfe [...fōōr eer-uh hilf-uh]

> *YOU MAY THEN HEAR*
> bitte schön, bitte sehr *you're welcome*

**that** dieser/diese/dieses [deez-er/deez-uh/deez-ess]

  **I would like that one** ich möchte das da [isH mursHtuh...]
  **how do you pronounce that?** wie spricht man das aus? [vee shprisHt man dass owss]
  **I think that...** ich glaube, dass... [isH glow-buh dass]

**the** der/die/das [dair/dee/dass]
**theatre** das Theater [tay-ah-ter]
**their** ihr/ihre/ihr [eer/eer-uh...]

  **their children** ihre Kinder

**theirs** ihre/ihre/ihres [eer-uh.../eer-ess]

> These forms correspond to the articles
> **der/die/das**. The plural is **ihre**.

**them** sie [zee]

  **I've lost them** ich habe sie verloren [isH hah-buh...fair-lor-ren]
  **I sent it to them** ich habe es *ihnen* geschickt [...ee-nen...]
  **for them** für sie [fōōr...]
  **with them** mit ihnen [...ee-nen]
  **who? – them** wer? – sie

**then** *(at that time)* damals
  *(after)* dann
**there** dort

**how do I get there?** wie komme ich dahin?
[vee komm-uh isн dah-hin]
**is there/are there…?** gibt es…? [gheept ess]
**there is/there are…** es gibt…
**there isn't/aren't…** es gibt kein/keine […kine/
kine-uh]
**there you are** *(giving)* hier, bitte! [heer bittuh]
**these** diese [deez-uh]
**they** sie [zee]
**thick** dick
*(stupid)* dumm [dɔɔm]
**thief** der Dieb [deep]
*(woman)* die Diebin [deebin]
**thigh** der Schenkel [sh-]
**thin** dünn [dɔɔn]
**thing** das Ding
**I've lost all my things** ich habe all meine
Sachen verloren [isн hah-buh al mine-uh zah-
кнen fair-lor-ren]
**think** denken
**I'll think it over** ich werde es mir überlegen [isн
vair-duh ess meer ōōber-lay-ghen]
**I think so** ich denke schon [isн denk-uh shohn]
**I don't think so** ich denke nicht […nisнt]
**third** *(adjective)* dritte [drit-uh]
**thirsty: I'm thirsty** ich habe Durst [isн hah-buh
dɔɔrst]
**this** dieser/diese/dieses [deez-er/deez-uh/deez-ess]
**can I have this one?** kann ich das haben?
[…dass hah-ben]
**this is my wife/this is Mr…** (das ist) meine
Frau/(das ist) Herr [mine-uh frow…]
**this is very good** das ist sehr gut […zair goot]
**this is…** *(on telephone)* hier ist… [heer ist]
**is this…?** ist das…?
**those** diese (da) [deez-uh (da)]
**no, not these, those!** nein, nicht diese,

(sondern) die da! [...zondern...]

**thread** der Faden [fah-den]

**throat** der Hals [halss]

**throttle** *(of motorbike)* der Gashebel [gahss-hay-bel]

**through** *(across)* durch [doorsн]

**throw** werfen [vairfen]

**thumb** der Daumen [dowmen]

**thunder** der Donner

**thunderstorm** ein Gewitter [gheh-vitter]

**Thursday** Donnerstag [donners-tahg]

**ticket** *(bus, train)* die Fahrkarte [-kartuh]
  *(plane)* das Ticket
  *(cinema)* die Eintrittskarte [ine-trits-kartuh]
  *(cloakroom etc)* die Garderobenmarke [gard-uh-ro-ben-mark-uh]

**tie** *(necktie)* die Krawatte [krav-at-uh]

**Tiefgarage** underground car park

**tight** *(clothes)* eng

**tights** *(pair)* die Strumpfhose [shtroompf-ho-zuh]

**time** die Zeit [tsite]
  **I haven't got time** ich habe keine Zeit [isн hah-buh kine-uh...]
  **for the time being** vorläufig [for-loyfisн]
  **this time/last time/next time** dieses Mal/letztes Mal/nächstes Mal [deez-ess mahl...]
  **three times** dreimal [dry-mahl]
  **have a good time!** viel Vergnügen! [feel fair-guh-noঁ-ghen]
  **what's the time?** wie spät ist es? [vee shpayt ist ess]

---

*HOW TO TELL THE TIME*
**it's one o'clock** es ist ein Uhr [...ine oor]
**it's two/three/four/five/six o'clock** es ist zwei/drei/vier/fünf/sechs Uhr [...tsvy/dry/feer/foঁnf/zeks...]

**it's 5/10/20 past seven** est ist fünf/zehn/zwanzig (Minuten) nach sieben […fŏŏnf/tsayn/tsvan-tsisн (minŏŏten) nahкн zeeben]
**it's 25 past seven** est ist fünf (Minuten) vor halb acht [...for halp ahкнt]
**it's 25 to eight** est ist fünf (Minuten) nach halb acht [...nahкн...]
**it's quarter past eight/eight fifteen** es ist Viertel nach acht/acht Uhr fünfzehn [...feertel nahкн ahкнt/ahкнt oor fŏŏnf-tsayn]
**it's half past nine/nine thirty** es ist halb zehn/neun Uhr dreißig [...halp tsayn/noyn oor dry-sisн]
**it's 25/20 to ten** es ist fünf/zehn nach halb zehn [...fŏŏnf/tsayn nahкн halp tsayn]
**it's 10/5 to eleven** es ist zehn/fünf (Minuten) vor elf [tsayn/fŏŏnf (minŏŏten) for...]
**it's quarter to eleven/10.45** es ist Viertel vor elf [...feertel for...]
**it's twelve o'clock (am/pm)** es ist zwölf (Uhr) [...tsvurlf...]
**at** um [oom]

Notice that, in German, half past **nine** etc is said as half **ten** etc.

**timetable** der Fahrplan [far-plahn]
**tin** *(can)* die Dose [dohzuh]
**tin-opener** der Dosenöffner [dohzen-urfner]
**tip** *(money)* ein Trinkgeld [-ghelt]
 **is the tip included?** ist das Trinkgeld inbegriffen?

✈ Tipping is broadly similar to the UK. But you're also expected to tip in pubs.

**tired** müde [mŏŏd-uh]

**I'm tired** ich bin müde [isH...]

**tissues** die Papiertaschentücher [pa-peer-tashen-tōōsH-er]

**to** zu [tsoo]

   **to Berlin/England** nach Berlin/England [nahKH...]

   *go to* **time**

> **Zu** used with **der** and **das** words usually becomes **zum**; with **die** words it becomes **zur**.
>
>    **to the station** zum Bahnhof [tsoom...]
>    **to the bank** zur Bank [tsoor...]

**toast** *(piece of)* ein Toast

**tobacco** der Tabak

**today** heute [hoytuh]

**toe** die Zehe [tsay-uh]

**together** zusammen [tsoo-zammen]

   **we're together** wir sind zusammen

   **can we pay all together?** können wir alles zusammen zahlen? [kurnen veer al-ess...tsah-len]

**toilet** die Toilette [twalet-uh]

   **where are the toilets?** wo sind die Toiletten? [vo zint dee...]

   **I have to go to the toilet** ich muss auf die Toilette [isH mooss owf dee...]

✈ Not very many public toilets in Germany; try the railway station; you can't use the toilet in a pub etc unless you're a customer.

**toilet paper: there's no toilet paper** es ist kein Toilettenpapier da [...kine twalet-en-pa-peer da]

**tomato** eine Tomate [tomah-tuh]

**tomato juice** der Tomatensaft [-zaft]

**tomato ketchup** der (Tomaten)ketchup

**tomorrow** morgen [mor-ghen]

**tomorrow morning** morgen früh [...frōō]
**tomorrow afternoon** morgen Nachmittag
[...nahкн-mitahg]
**tomorrow evening** morgen Abend [...ah-
bent]
  **the day after tomorrow** übermorgen [ōōber-]
  **see you tomorrow** bis morgen
**tongue** die Zunge [tsōōng-uh]
**tonic (water)** das Tonic(water)
**tonight** heute Abend [hoytuh ah-bent]
**tonsillitis** die Mandelentzündung [mandel-ent-
tsōōn-dōong]
**too** zu [tsoo]
  *(also)* auch [owкн]
  **that's too much** das ist zu viel [dass ist tsoo
  feel]
  **me too** ich auch [isн owкн]
**tool** das Werkzeug [vairk-tsoyg]
**tooth** der Zahn [tsahn]
**toothache: I've got toothache** ich habe
Zahnschmerzen [isн hah-buh tsahn-shmairtsen]
**toothbrush** eine Zahnbürste [tsahn-bōōrst-uh]
**toothpaste** die Zahnpasta [tsahn-]
**top: on top of** auf [owf]
  **at the top** oben [o-ben]
  **on the top floor** im obersten Stock [...shtock]
**torch** eine Taschenlampe [tashen-lamp-uh]
**total** die Endsumme [ent-zōōm-uh]
**tough** *(meat, person)* zäh [tsay]
**tour** *(of area)* die Rundreise [rōōnt-ry-zuh]
  *(of town)* die Rundfahrt
  *(on foot)* der Rundgang
  **we'd like to go on a tour of...** wir möchten
  gerne eine Rundreise/eine Rundfahrt/einen
  Rundgang durch...machen [veer mursнten
  gairn...mahкнen]
  **we're touring around** wir reisen herum [veer

ry-zen hair-com]

**tourist** der Tourist [too-rist]
  *(woman)* die Touristin
  **I'm a tourist** ich bin Tourist

**tourist office** das Fremdenverkehrsbüro [frem-den-fair-kairs-bōoro]

**tow** abschleppen [ap-shleppen]
  **can you give me a tow?** könnten Sie mich abschleppen? [kurnten zee mish...]

**towards** gegen [gay-ghen]
  **he was coming straight towards me** er kam geradewegs auf mich zu [air kahm gheh-rah-duh-vaygs owf mish tsoo]

**towel** das Handtuch [hant-tooкн]

**town** die Stadt [shtat]
  **in town** in der Stadt
  **would you take me into town?** würden Sie mich in die Stadt bringen? [vōorden zee mish...]

**towrope** das Abschleppseil [ap-shlep-zile]

**traditional** traditionell [tradits-yonel]
  **a traditional German meal** ein echt deutsches Essen [ine esht doytshess...]

**traffic** der Verkehr [fair-kair]

**traffic jam** ein Stau [shtow]

**traffic lights** die Ampel

**train** der Zug [tsoog]

✈ Tickets should be bought before boarding, either from a machine or at the ticket desk; it is possible to buy a ticket on the train as well but expect a surcharge for this. If you're travelling Intercity make sure you buy your Zuschlag [tsoo-shlahg] (supplement) first.

> *YOU MAY HEAR*
> noch jemand zugestiegen? *any more tickets?*

**trainers** die Turnschuhe [toorn-shoo-uh]
**train station** der Bahnhof [bahn-hohff]
**tram** die Straßenbahn [shtrahssen-bahn]

> ✈ You normally get a ticket from the ticket
> machine at the tram stop. Don't forget to
> punch it in another machine on the tram.

**tranquillizers** die Beruhigungsmittel [buh-roo-
igoongs-]
**translate** übersetzen [ōōber-zet-sen]
  **would you translate that for me?** würden Sie
  das für mich übersetzen? [vōōrden zee dass fōōr
  misH…]
**travel** reisen [ry-zen]
**travel agent's** das Reisebüro [ry-zuh-bōōro]
**traveller's cheque** der Travellerscheck
**tree** der Baum [bowm]
**tremendous** *(very good)* enorm [ay-norm]
**trim: just a trim, please** nur nachschneiden,
bitte [noor nahKH-shnyden bittuh]
**trip** *(journey)* eine Reise [ry-zuh]
  *(outing)* der Ausflug [owss-floog]
  **we want to go on a trip to…** wir möchten
  nach…fahren [veer mursHten nahKH…]
**trouble** die Schwierigkeiten [shvee-risH-kite-en]
  **I'm having trouble with…** ich habe
  Schwierigkeiten mit… [isH hah-buh…]
**trousers** die Hose [ho-zuh]
**true** wahr [vahr]
  **it's not true** das ist nicht wahr [dass ist nisHt…]
**trunks** *(swimming)* die Badehose [bah-duh-ho-zuh]
**try** versuchen [fair-zooKH-en]
  **can I try it on?** kann ich es anprobieren? [kan
  isH ess an-pro-beeren]

**T-shirt** das 'T-Shirt'
**Tuesday** Dienstag [deenz-tahg]
**tunnel** der Tunnel [t∞nel]
**Turkey** die Türkei [t∞rkı]
**Turkish** türkisch [t∞rkish]
**turn: where do we turn off?** wo biegen wir ab?
[vo bee-ghen veer ap]
**twice** zweimal [tsvy-mal]
  **twice as much** doppelt soviel [...zo-feel]
**twin beds** zwei (Einzel)betten [tsvy (ine-tsel)-]
**twin room** ein Zweibettzimmer [tsvy bet-tsimmer]
**typical** typisch [t∞-pish]
**tyre** der Reifen [ry-fen]
  **I need a new tyre** ich brauche einen neuen
  Reifen [isн browкн-uh ine-en noy-en...]

✈ **tyre pressure**

| lb/sq in | 18 | 20 | 22 | 26 | 28 | 30 |
|---|---|---|---|---|---|---|
| kg/sq cm | 1.3 | 1.4 | 1.5 | 1.7 | 2 | 2.1 |

# U [oo]

**U-Bahn** underground
**ugly** hässlich [hess-lisн]
**ulcer** das Geschwür [gheh-shv∞r]
**umbrella** der Schirm [sheerm]
**Umleitung** diversion
**umsteigen** change
**uncle: my uncle** mein Onkel
**uncomfortable** unbequem [∞n-buh-kvaym]
**unconscious** bewusstlos [buh-v∞st-lohss]
**under** unter [∞nter]
**underdone** nicht gar [nisнт...]
**underground** *(rail)* die U-Bahn [oo-bahn]

✈ Make sure you stamp your ticket before
  getting on the train, usually in a machine

on or near the platforms, sometimes even
on the train itself.

**understand: I understand** ich verstehe [isH fair-
shtay-uh]
  **I don't understand** das verstehe ich nicht
[...nisHt]
  **do you understand?** verstehen Sie?/verstehst
du? *(polite/familiar)* [fair-shtay-en zee...]
**undo** aufmachen [owf-mahkHen]
**unfriendly** unfreundlich [oon-froynt-lisH]
**unhappy** unglücklich [oon-glöck-lisH]
**United States** die Vereinigten Staaten [fair-ine-
isH-ten shtah-ten]
**university** die Universität [oonivairsitayt]
**unleaded** bleifreies Benzin [bly-fry-ess ben-tseen]
**unlock** aufschließen [owf-shleessen]
**untersagt** prohibited
**until** bis
  **until next year** bis nächstes Jahr [...nekstess...]
  **not until Tuesday** nicht vor Dienstag [nisHt
for...]
**unusual** ungewöhnlich [oon-gheh-vurn-lisH]
**up** oben [o-ben]
  **he's not up yet** er ist noch nicht auf [air ist
nokH nisHt owf]
  **what's up?** was ist los? [vass ist lohss]
  **up there** da oben
**upside-down** verkehrt herum [fair-kairt hair-oom]
**upstairs** oben [o-ben]
**urgent** dringend [dring-ent]
**us** uns [oonss]
  **it's us** wir sind's [veer zints]
  **with/for us** mit/für uns
  **who? – us** wer? – wir
**USA** die USA [oo-ess-ah]
**use: can I use...?** kann ich...benutzen? [kan isH

buh-n∞t-sen]
**useful** nützlich [n∞ts-lisн]
**usual** gewöhnlich [gheh-vurn-lisн]
 **as usual** wie gewöhnlich [vee...]
**usually** normalerweise [normahler-vyzuh]
**U-turn** die Wende [ven-duh]

# V [fow]

**vacate** *(room)* räumen [roy-men]
**vacation** die Ferien [fay-ree-en]
**vaccination** die Impfung [imp-foong]
**vacuum flask** eine Thermosflasche [tairmos-flash-uh]
**valid** gültig [g∞ltisн]
 **how long is it valid for?** wie lange gilt es? [vee lang-uh ghilt ess]
**valley** das Tal [tahl]
**valuable** wertvoll [vairt-fol]
 **will you look after my valuables?** würden Sie meine Wertsachen für mich aufbewahren? [v∞rden zee mine-uh vairt-zaкнen f∞r misн owf-buh-varen]
**value** der Wert [vairt]
**van** der Kombi
**vanilla** Vanille [van-ee-luh]
**veal** das Kalbfleisch [kalp-flysh]
**vegetables** die Gemüse [gheh-m∞-zuh]
**vegetarian** vegetarisch [vay-gheh-taнrish]
**ventilator** der Ventilator [-laн-tor]
**verboten** forbidden
**Verkauf...** selling rate...
**Verspätung** delay
**very** sehr [zair]
 **very much** sehr
**via** über [∞ber]
**village** das Dorf

**vine** die Rebe [ray-buh]
**vinegar** der Essig [-isH]
**vineyard** der Weinberg [vine-bairk]
**violent** heftig [-isH]
**visit** *(verb)* besuchen [buh-zooKH-en]
**vodka** der Wodka [v-]
**voice** die Stimme [shtim-uh]
**voltage** die Spannung [shpan-oong]

✈ 220 in Germany, as in the UK.

**Vorsicht!** caution
**Vorsicht, bissiger Hund** beware of the dog
**Vorstellung** performance

# W [vay]

**waist** die Taille [ty-yuh]
**wait: will we have to wait long?** müssen wir
  lange warten? [m00ssen veer lang-uh varten]
  **wait for me** warte auf mich [...owf misH]
  **I'm waiting for a friend/my wife** ich warte auf
  einen Freund/meine Frau [isH var-tuh owf ine-en
  froynt/mine-uh frow]
**waiter** der Kellner
  **waiter!** (Herr) Ober!
**waitress** die Kellnerin
**wake: will you wake me up at 7.30?** wecken Sie
  mich bitte um 7.30? [vecken zee misH bittuh oom
  halp ahkHt]
**Wales** Wales [v-]
**walk: can we walk there?** können wir zu Fuß
  hingehen? [kurnen veer tsoo fooss hin-gay-en]
**walking shoes** die Wanderschuhe [van-der-shoo-uh]
**wall** die Mauer [mow-er]
  *(inside)* die Wand [vant]
**wallet** die Brieftasche [breef-tash-uh]
**want: I want a...** ich möchte ein... [isH

murSHtuh]
**I want to talk to...** ich möchte mit...sprechen
[...shpresHen]
**what do you want?** was möchten Sie? [vass
murSHten zee ]
**I don't want to** ich will nicht [isH vil nisHt]
**he/she wants to...** er/sie will... [air/zee vil]
**war** der Krieg [kreeg]
**warm** warm [varm]
**warning** eine Warnung [varn-∞ng]
Wartesaal waiting room
**was**

> Here is the past tense of the German verb
> 'to be'.
>
> **I was** ich war [isH var]
> **you were** *(singular familiar)* du warst [doo
> varst]
> **you were** *(singular polite)* Sie waren [zee
> varen]
> **he/she/it was** er/sie/es war [air/zee/ess...]
> **we were** wir waren [veer...]
> **you were** *(plural familiar)* ihr wart [eer vart]
> **you were** *(plural polite)* Sie waren
> **they were** sie waren

**wash: can you wash these for me?** könnten Sie
diese für mich waschen? [kurnten zee dee-zuh
foor misH vashen]
**washbasin** ein Waschbecken [vash-becken]
**washer** *(for nut)* die Dichtung [disH-t∞ng]
**washing machine** die Waschmachine [vash-mash-
een-uh]
**washing powder** das Waschpulver [vash-p∞lver]
**wasp** die Wespe [vesp-uh]
**watch** *(wristwatch)* die (Armband)uhr
[(armbant)oor]

**will you watch my bags for me?** würden Sie für mich auf meine Taschen aufpassen? [vōōrden zee fōōr misH owf...owf-pas-en]

**watch out!** Achtung! [ahкH-tōong]

**water** das Wasser [vasser]

**can I have some water?** kann ich etwas Wasser haben? [kan isH etvass...hah-ben]

**hot and cold running water** fließend kalt und warm Wasser [flee-sent...]

**waterfall** der Wasserfall [vasser-fal]

**waterproof** wasserdicht [vasser-disHt]

**way** der Weg [vayg]

**it's this way** es ist hier entlang [ess ist heer...]

**it's that way** es ist da entlang

**is it on the way to...?** liegt es auf dem Weg nach...? [leegt ess owf daym vayg nahкH]

**no way!** auf keinen Fall! [owf kine-en fal]

**do it this way** machen Sie es so [mahкHen zee ess zo]

**could you tell me the way to get to...?** könnten Sie mir sagen, wie ich nach ..., komme? [kurnten zee meer zah-ghen vee isH nahкH...kommuh]

*go to* **where** *for answers*

**we** wir [veer]

**weak** schwach [shvahкH]

**weather** das Wetter [v-]

**what filthy weather!** so ein Mistwetter! [zo ine...]

**what's the weather forecast?** was sagt der Wetterbericht? [vas zahgt dair -buh-risHt]

> *YOU MAY THEN HEAR*
> überwiegend heiter *generally fine*
> leichte/schwere Schauer *light/heavy showers*
> Gewitter *thunderstorms*
> sonnig *sunny*
> kalt *cold*

**website** eine 'Website'

**Wechselstube** bureau de change

**Wednesday** Mittwoch [mit-voKH]

**week** die Woche [voKH-uh]

  **a week today** heute in einer Woche [hoytuh in ine-er...]

  **a week tomorrow** morgen in einer Woche [mor-ghen...]

**weekend: at the weekend** am Wochenende [...voKHen-end-uh]

**weight** das Gewicht [gheh-visHt]

**welcome: you're welcome** bitte sehr [bittuh zair]

**well: I'm not feeling well** ich fühle mich nicht wohl [isH fööl-uh misH nisHt vohl]

  **he's not well** es geht ihm nicht gut [ess gayt eem nisHt goot]

  **how are you? – very well, thanks** wie geht's? – danke, gut! [vee gayts – dankuh goot]

  **you speak English very well** Sie sprechen sehr gut Englisch [zee shpresHen zair goot eng-lish]

  **well, well!** das gibt's ja nicht [...gheepts ya nisHt]

**Welsh** walisisch [val-ee-zish]

**were** *go to* **was**

**west** der Westen [v-]

**West Indies** die Westindischen Inseln [vest-indishen inzeln]

**wet** nass [nass]

**what?** was? [vass]

  **what is that?** was ist das?

  **what for?** wozu? [vo-tsoo]

  **what train?** welcher Zug? [velsher...]

**wheel** das Rad [raht]

**wheel chair** der Rollstuhl [rol-shtool]

**when?** wann? [van]

  **when we arrived** als wir ankamen [alss veer an-kahmen]

**where?** wo? [vo]
  **where is...?** wo ist...?

> *YOU MAY THEN HEAR*
> geradeaus *straight ahead*
> erste Querstraße links/rechts *first left/right*
> an der Ampel vorbei *past the traffic lights*
> gehen Sie zurück bis... *go back to...*

**which?** welcher/welche/welches? [velsher...]

> *YOU MAY THEN HEAR*
> dieser/diese/dieses *this one*
> der da/die da/das da *that one there*
> der/die/das linke *the one on the left*

**whisky** ein Whisky [v-]
**white** weiß [vice]
**white wine** ein Weißwein [vice-vine]
**Whitsun** Pfingsten
**who?** wer? [vair]
**whose: whose is this?** wem gehört das? [vaym
gheh-hurt dass]

> *YOU MAY THEN HEAR*
> (das gehört) ihm *(it belongs) to him*
> ihr *to her*
> mir *it's mine*

**why?** warum? [varoom]
  **why not?** warum nicht? [...nisHt]

> *YOU MAY THEN HEAR*
> weil *because*

**wide** weit [vite]
**wife: my wife** meine Frau [mine-uh frow]
**will: when will it be finished?** wann ist es fertig?
  [van ist ess fairtisH]
  **I'll come back** ich komme wieder [isH kom-uh
  veeder]

**win** gewinnen [gheh-vinnen]
  **who won?** wer hat gewonnen? [vair...]
**wind** der Wind [vint]
**window** das Fenster
  **near the window** am Fenster
**window seat** ein Fensterplatz
**windscreen** die Windschutzscheibe [vint-shoots-shy-buh]
**windscreen wipers** die Scheibenwischer [shy-ben-visher]
**windy** windig [vindisн]
**wine** der Wein [vine]
  **can I see the wine list?** kann ich die Weinkarte haben? [kan isн dee vine-kartuh hah-ben]
  **two red wines** zwei Gläser Rotwein [...glayzer...]

✈ Mainly white wines (**Weißwein** [vice-vine]) and fewer reds (**Rotwein** [roht-vine]). There are three quality grades:

**Tafelwein** is a table wine without a named vineyard;
**Qualitätswein** is quality wine from a designated region;
**Qualitätswein mit Prädikat** is top-of-the-range quality wine.

There are countless varieties and some of the main grapes are:
**Riesling** medium dry;
**Sylvaner** dry;
**Gutedel** very dry;
**Müller-Thurgau** light, fruity;
**Ruländer** full-bodied, sweetish;
**Traminer** full-bodied, strong;
**Weißherbst** and **Schiller** are fruity rosés (**Rosé**).

Some wine terms:
lieblich *sweet*
halbtrocken *medium*
trocken *dry*

If you like your wine really dry, ask for it
**herb** [hairp].

**winter** der Winter [v-]
**wire** der Draht
  *(electric)* die Leitung [ly-toong]
**wish: best wishes** alles Gute! [al-ess gootuh]
  *(on letter)* herzliche Grüße [hairts-lisнuh grœ̄-
  suh]
**with** mit
**without** ohne [o-nuh]
**witness** ein Zeuge [tsoy-guh]
  *(woman)* eine Zeugin
  **will you act as a witness for me?** darf ich Sie
  als Zeugen/Zeugin nennen? [...isн zee alss tsoy-
  ghen...]
**woman** die Frau [frow]
  **women** die Frauen [frowen]
**wonderful** herrlich [hair-lisн]
**won't: it won't start** es springt nicht an [ess
  shpringt nisнt an]
**wood** das Holz [holts]
  *(forest)* der Wald [valt]
**wool** die Wolle [vol-uh]
**word** das Wort [vort]
  **I don't know that word** ich kenne das Wort
  nicht [isн ken-uh dass...nisнt]
**work** arbeiten [ar-by-ten]
  **I work in London** ich arbeite in London [isн ar-
  by-tuh...]
  **it's not working** es funktioniert nicht [ess fœnk-
  tsee-o-neert nisнt]

**worry: I'm worried about him** ich mache mir Sorgen um ihn [isH mahкHuh meer zor-ghen oom een]

**don't worry** keine Sorge [kine-uh...]

**worse: it's worse** es ist schlimmer [...shl-]

**worst** schlechteste [shlesHt-est-uh]

**worth: it's not worth that much** so viel ist es nicht wert [zo feel ist ess nisHt vairt]

**worthwhile: is it worthwhile going to...?** lohnt es sich, nach...zu gehen? [...zisH nahкH...tsoo gay-en]

**wrap: could you wrap it up?** könnten Sie es einpacken? [kurnten zee ess ine-packen]

**wrench** *(tool)* ein Schraubenschlüssel [shrowben-shlōosel]

**wrist** das Handgelenk [hant-gheh-lenk]

**write** schreiben [shry-ben]

**could you write it down?** könnten Sie das aufschreiben? [kurnten zee dass owf-shry-ben]

**I'll write to you** ich schreibe Ihnen [isH shry-buh ee-nen ]

**writing paper** das Schreibpapier [shryp-pa-peer]

**wrong** falsch [falsh]

**I think the bill's wrong** ich glaube, die Rechnung stimmt nicht [isH glow-buh dee resH-noong shtimt nisHt]

**there's something wrong with...** da stimmt etwas nicht mit... [...etvass...]

**you're wrong** Sie irren sich [zee irren zisH] *(familiar)* du irrst dich

**that's the wrong key** das ist der falsche Schlüssel

**sorry, wrong number** tut mir leid, falsch verbunden [toot meer lite falsh fair-boonden]

**I got the wrong train** ich habe den falschen Zug genommen

**what's wrong?** was ist los? [vass ist lohss]

# Y [ɔɔpsilon]

**yacht** die Jacht [yahкнт]
**yard**

✈ 1 yard = 91.44 cms = 0.91 m

**year** das Jahr [y-]
  **this year** dieses Jahr [deez-ess...]
  **next year** nächstes Jahr [nekstess...]
**yellow** gelb [ghelp]
**yellow pages** die Gelben Seiten [ghelben zy-ten]
**yes** ja [ya]

> To disagree with a statement containing a
> 'not' you should use the word **doch**.
>   **you can't – yes, I can** Sie können das
>   nicht – doch! [zee kurnen dass nisнт
>   – doкн]

**yesterday** gestern [ghestern]
  **the day before yesterday** vorgestern [for-]
  **yesterday morning** gestern Morgen
  **yesterday afternoon** gestern Nachmittag
  [...naнкн-mitahg]
**yet: is it ready yet?** ist es *schon* fertig? [ist ess
  shohn fairtisн]
  **not yet** noch nicht [noкн nisнт]
**yoghurt** ein Joghurt [yo-gɶort]
**you** Sie [zee]

> This word can be used for talking to one
> or several people. It changes to **Ihnen** in
> some cases.
>   **is that you?** sind Sie das?
>   **I can't hear you** ich höre Sie nicht
>   **I'll send it to you** ich schicke es *Ihnen*
>   [...ee-nen]

**with you** mit Ihnen
**for you** für Sie

There is also another word for 'you' – **du** [doo] – (called the 'familiar form') which you can use with people you know well or, say, if you are a student, with other students. Don't use it with strangers like bus drivers, receptionists etc. It changes to **dich** or **dir** in some cases.

**is that you?** bist du's?
**I can't hear you** ich höre dich nicht
[...dɪsH...]
**I'll send it to you** ich schicke es dir
[...deer]
**with you** mit dir
**for you** für dich

This **du** form has a plural – **ihr** (which changes to **euch** in some cases).

**is that you?** seid ihr's? [zite eerss]
**I can't hear you** ich höre euch nicht
[...oysH...]
**I'll send it to you** ich schicke es euch
**with/for you** mit/für euch

**young** jung [yɔɔng]
**your**

The German for 'your' will depend on which word for 'you' is being used.
*(with Sie)* Ihr/Ihre/Ihr [eer/eer-uh...]
*(with du)* dein/deine/dein [dine/dine-uh...]
*(with ihr)* euer/eure/euer [oy-er/oy-ruh...]

The three forms of each correspond to the articles **der/die/das**. Plurals are **Ihre**, **deine** and **eure**.

**yours** Ihrer; deiner; eurer [eer-er; dine-er; oy-rer]
**youth hostel** eine Jugendherberge [yoo-ghent-hair-bair-guh]

✈ Only Bavaria has an age limit of 27 for people travelling alone.

# Z [tset]

**zero** Null [nool]
   **below zero** unter Null [oonter...]
**ziehen** pull
**Zimmer frei** vacancies, rooms
**zip** der Reißverschluss [rice-fair-shlooss]
   **could you put a new zip on?** könnten Sie einen neuen Reißverschluss anbringen? [kurnten zee ine-en noy-en...an-bringen]
**Zoll** Customs
**Zutritt verboten** no admission, keep out
**zu verkaufen** for sale
**zu vermieten** for hire, to let

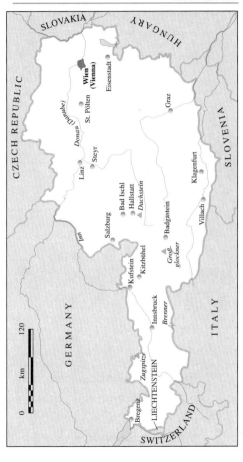

AUSTRIA

LIECHTENSTEIN

G E R M A N Y

I T A L Y

F R A N C E

Inn

Klosters

Davos

Arosa

Chur

St. Moritz

St. Gallen

Flims

St. Gotthard

Locarno

Lugano

Luganer See

Ascona

Lago Maggiore

Zürich

Zug

Zuger See

Luzern (Lucerne)

Vierwaldstättersee (Lake Lucerne)

Brienzer See

Grindelwald

Eiger

Rhein (Rhine)

Rhein (Rhine)

Aare

Basel (Basle)

Bern

Interlaken

Thuner See

Crans Montana

Saas Fee

Gstaad

Sion

Verbier

Zermatt

Matterhorn

Leysin

Les Diablerets

Lausanne

Montreux

Villars

Rhône

Genfer See (Lake Geneva)

Genf (Geneva)

km

0    90

# Numbers

| | | |
|---|---|---|
| 0 | null [nool] | |
| 1 | eins [ine-ss] | |
| 2 | zwei [tsvy] | |
| 3 | drei [dry] | |
| 4 | vier [feer] | |
| 5 | fünf [foonf] | |
| 6 | sechs [zeks] | |
| 7 | sieben [zeeben] | |
| 8 | acht [ahкнт] | |
| 9 | neun [noyn] | |
| 10 | zehn [tsayn] | |
| 11 | elf | |
| 12 | zwölf [tsvurlf] | |
| 13 | dreizehn [dry-tsayn] | |
| 14 | vierzehn | |
| 15 | fünfzehn | |
| 16 | sechzehn | |
| 17 | siebzehn [zeep-tsayn] | |
| 18 | achtzehn | |
| 19 | neunzehn | |
| 20 | zwanzig [tsvantsisн] | |
| 21 | einundzwanzig [ine-oont-tsvantsisн] | |
| 22 | zweiundzwanzig | |
| 23 | dreiundzwanzig | |
| 24 | vierundzwanzig | |
| 25 | fünfundzwanzig | |
| 26 | sechsundzwanzig | |
| 27 | siebenundzwanzig | |
| 28 | achtundzwanzig | |
| 29 | neunundzwanzig | |
| 30 | dreißig [dry-sisн] | |
| 40 | vierzig [feertsisн] | |
| 50 | fünfzig | |
| 60 | sechzig | |
| 70 | siebzig [zeep-tsisн] | |

| | |
|---|---|
| **80** | achtzig |
| **90** | neunzig |
| **100** | (ein)hundert [(ine)hɔɔndert] |
| **101** | (ein)hunderteins |
| **165** | (ein)hundertfünfundsechzig |
| **200** | zweihundert |
| **1,000** | (ein)tausend [(ine)-tow-zent] |
| **2,000** | zweitausend |
| **4,653** | viertausendsechshundertdreiundfünfzig |
| **1,000,000** | eine Million [ine-uh mil-yohn] |

*NB in Germany a comma is used for a decimal point; for thousands use a full stop, eg 3.000*

## The alphabet: how to spell in German

**a** [ah]  **b** [bay]  **c** [tsay]  **d** [day]  **e** [ay]  **f** [eff]
**g** [gay]  **h** [hah]  **i** [ee]  **j** [yot]  **k** [kah]  **l** [el]
**m** [em]  **n** [en]  **o** [oh]  **p** [pay]  **q** [koo]  **r** [air]
**s** [ess]  **t** [tay]  **u** [oo]  **v** [fow]  **w** [vay]  **x** [iks]
**y** [ɔɔpsilon]  **z** [tset]

The German letter **ß** is equivalent to **ss**.